CW00350917

MANAGING
THE
PLANET

MANAGING
THE
PLANET

THE POLITICS OF THE NEW MILLENNIUM

NORMAN MOSS

Earthscan Publications Ltd, London

First published in the UK in 2000 by
Earthscan Publications Ltd

Copyright © Norman Moss, 2000

A catalogue record for this book is available from the British Library

ISBN: 1 85383 644 3

Typesetting by JS Typesetting, Wellingborough, Northants
Printed and bound by Creative Print and Design Wales, Ebbw Vale
Cover design by Susanne Harris

For a full list of publications please contact:

Earthscan Publications Ltd
120 Pentonville Road
London, N1 9JN, UK
Tel: +44 (0)20 7278 0433
Fax: +44 (0)20 7278 1142
Email: earthinfo@earthscan.co.uk
http://www.earthscan.co.uk

Earthscan is an editorially independent subsidiary of Kogan Page Ltd
and publishes in association with WWF-UK and the International
Institute for Environment and Development

This book is printed on elemental chlorine-free paper

For Hilary, who wanted me to write this

CONTENTS

INTRODUCTION

IN THE SECOND half of the 20th century, history entered a new phase. The human race became so numerous, and its technical power so great, that its activities began to have an impact on the biosphere, the entire planet. In the last quarter of the 20th century people realized that this was happening and began to address the problems it raised.

If the impact on the biosphere is not to be too damaging, these activities must be controlled. Since all nations live in the biosphere and all can affect it, all must be involved. This is an entirely new kind of international situation, and one that will become increasingly important. It will change the ways that nations deal with one another, and it will change the way we live.

Drawing attention to the threat to the planetary environment, the environmentalist Donella Meadows and two co-authors wrote: 'The world will decide which direction to take.'[1] This is the kind of statement we hear often from environmentalists. Jeremy Rifkin writes: 'The choice of whether we live or die is in our hands. Mankind must make up its mind what kind of future it wants.'[2]

Such statements are well-intentioned but they are literally nonsense. They do not make sense. The world cannot decide anything. Mankind is a biological entity but not a political entity. It has no mind to make up, no collective will to reach a decision or carry one out.

Groups of human beings take decisions and make up their minds, not the whole human race; nations are usually the most conspicuous and important of these groups although by no means the only ones. Nations and other groups can act together purposefully to control the planetary environment. Acting together involves conflict, compromises and the reconciling of conflicting views and interests – in other words, politics.

The most important single threat today to the planetary environment is the warming of the earth due to human activities. We are seeing some of the effects and we will see more. Worryingly, there is much uncertainty about what future effects there will be. Governments have reached agreement on the first stage of stemming the warming process although negotiation continues, particularly on methods for achieving this. If or when this is worked out governments will have to negotiate the next stage.

In these negotiations, new and unfamiliar alliances are springing up. Powerful countries are finding that they have to buy, in one form or another, the cooperation of countries that are less powerful. New mechanisms to deal with the problem and new forms of cooperation are emerging, as they did to deal with the global problem of ozone layer depletion. These negotiations are ongoing. Progress will depend on the ability of governments to agree: on the impact of climate change, which acts as a spur to action; on developments in technology, which will determine what can be done and at what cost; and on business, which will decide where the profits lie. This is where politics, technology, economics and the environment all meet.

Attempts to grapple with these problems are ushering in a new kind of politics. The issue is not what nations do to each other but what they do to the planet. Its task, increasingly, will be the management of the planet.

A planetary environmental problem erodes national sovereignty. A fundamental feature of sovereignty is the ability of a nation to defend itself. Climate change threatens to damage most nations, probably all. No nation alone can defend itself against this threat, not even the most powerful. What other nations do affects the climate. We are all dependent on the actions of others.

There is a parallel here with the advent of nuclear weapons. This also introduced something new into international relations. No country can defend itself against nuclear attack. Its safety depends on international agreements, explicit or tacit, and the restraint of others (mutual deterrence being a form of tacit agreement).

This new situation raises questions of values, of our attitude to our natural environment and our place within it, and to the rights of future generations as compared with our own.

People have changed the environment ever since the advent of agriculture, usually unwittingly, turning savannas into deserts, destroying forests, silting up rivers and wiping out species. Since the coming of civilization they have done so on a scale that crosses international borders. Governments have had to negotiate international environmental agreements. But planet-wide impact is something new. We are at one of the watersheds of history, comparable to the agricultural revolution 10,000 years ago and the Industrial Revolution 300 years ago.

With the information available, we can now look at the earth as a whole. We can see that the planet appears to be coming within sight of the limits of its resources. World food production has multiplied during this century but population continues to increase and more people demand more and more expensive food. Fish are being caught and eaten faster than they can be replenished. Water use has increased beyond its sustainable level, while demand grows for industry, agriculture and increasingly modern homes. Industrial activities are putting strains on the environment that cannot be maintained.

We can look at these as global problems, but governments try to deal with them in the traditional way, as national problems. Each government is concerned to ensure that there is enough for its own people or, sometimes, just for members of the government and their friends – what is called the national interest. That is what national governments have always done and that is what they were set up to do. This is why, when one looks not only at the amount of resources but also at their distribution, the inequality is so striking: malnutrition the norm in some areas while in others obesity due to over-eating is a national concern.

But the problems of the planetary environment cannot be dealt with in the traditional way. Governments cannot simply look after their own interests. They have to look at these issues globally.

Planet-wide environmental damage is something new. Climate change is the most urgent issue. There are others, among which the loss of biodiversity is the most important, and there will be more. Genetic engineering is likely to produce new kinds of problems. The exploitation of outer space can have an impact on the whole planet. Other activities in chemistry and biotechnology may have side-effects that will come as a surprise, much as the hole in the ozone layer and the greenhouse effect did. What has produced the reduction in male sperm count that has been observed in several countries? Already some new problems are glimpsed on the horizon.

While talks on climate change are going on, the world is getting warmer. We are pouring gases into the atmosphere at a rate that continues to heat up the planet. But the rate is being reduced.

Like some gigantic supertanker, the world is changing course, very slowly. New ways of thinking are emerging. The new technologies that will change our lives have made their appearance.

The aim of governments when they negotiate on this topic is to bring down further the emission of greenhouse gases. Ultimately, it is to set up a global programme to reduce these emissions in which every country will take part. The need is urgent. But these negotiations are not the only area of action. Business, technology and consumers are all playing a part, and in some areas are making the running.

These international negotiations are open-ended, and they are designed to be. The problem of controlling climate change is not one that can be solved once and for all. Solutions will have to be found far into the future, in fact, insofar as we can use the term about humanity, forever. The climatic disasters that must be avoided in the 21st century must be avoided in future centuries also. To focus on just one effect of global warming, sea level rise. No one knows what the world will be like 300 years from now, but it seems likely that New York will still be there, and so will London, Tokyo, Sydney and Bombay. All these cities and many others will be inundated if sea levels rise. Their inhabitants will want to save them as they do today.

Once again there is a comparison with nuclear weapons. We have lived with them for more than half a century and managed to avoid a nuclear holocaust. But nuclear weapons, at least in their potential, are here forever. The problem of living with them is one that every future generation will have to deal with.

The age of ideological politics that began in the 17th century is drawing to a close. In the centuries to come, the age of planetary politics, of managing Spaceship Earth, will be a part of what replaces it. Our numbers will become greater, barring some global catastrophe, and our technological power will increase, opening up new avenues for environmental impact. These will play a significant part in human affairs in the millennium that is now beginning.

The way that nations deal with the problem of climate change will point to the way other planetary issues will be treated in the future. This is the new kind politics, the politics of the planet.

1

MIDGLEY'S CHILDREN

Human civilisation is now the dominant cause of change in the global environment – Al Gore[1]

a world of made is not a world of born – e e cummings[2]

ASK A HISTORIAN to name the people who have changed our world in the 20th century. He or she will probably name some world leaders, major thinkers whose ideas have had an impact, some scientists, some inventors and perhaps some creators of popular culture. It is unlikely that the name of Thomas Midgley Jr will feature on the list. Yet in a very real sense Thomas Midgley changed the world in a way that no statesman or major thinker did. These merely changed the lives of a lot of people who live in the world. They did not leave their mark on the planet in the way that Thomas Midgley left his.

He was a chemist who lived in America in the first decades of the 20th century. He had a distinguished career. He was awarded citations and medals for achievements in his field, he was a member

of the board of directors of the American Chemical Society from
1930 to 1944, and its president in 1944.

As a young man in 1917 Midgley worked in the Dayton Engineering Laboratory in Dayton, Ohio, where the Delco automobile
engine was being developed. He was given a problem concerning
petrol, or gasoline. Before that time, petrol engines were used mostly
to power electric generators in rural homes. Now their principal
use was to power the automobiles that were being produced in
quantity. But the petrol knocked, that is, instead of burning smoothly
it had a tendency to pre-ignite, making a pop-pop sound. This did
not matter in a power generator, but in an automobile it made for
a jerky, uncomfortable motion and inefficient fuel use.

Midgley's solution, which he arrived at in 1921, was to add
lead to the petrol, in a new compound, tetra-ethyl lead. He had a
flair for exposition, and he demonstrated his discovery proudly to
a meeting of the American Chemical Society on the stage of the
Carnegie Music Hall in Pittsburgh. The first petrol containing tetra-
ethyl lead, manufactured under licence, went on sale in garages in
Dayton in 1923, and soon it was being sold all over the world. For
the next 60 years cars and trucks, eventually numbering hundreds
of millions, used petrol with Midgley's additive.

As cars filled city streets, the lead content in the atmosphere
mounted. In 1920, the air in an average American or European city
contained less than a tenth of a microgram of lead per cubic metre,
barely enough to be detected by instruments. In 1970, before
unleaded petrol was introduced, the air in New York City contained
3.2 micrograms of lead per cubic metre, more than 30 times as much.
This was enough, as we know today, to damage the lungs and nerve
cells of the inhabitants. Lead still pollutes the air in many cities today.

The change was not limited to traffic-clogged cities. It has
permeated the atmosphere of the entire planet. On the Greenland

ice cap, a thousand miles from any major road, scientists digging down can date the layers of ice from the 1920s onward by the lead content of the air trapped inside. Thomas Midgley changed the atmosphere of the world.

His impact on our planet did not end there. He went to work on other projects, and in the late 1920s, working now for General Motors Frigidaire, he took up another challenge. Electric refrigerators were replacing the old ice boxes. They work by putting a liquid into the circulatory system under pressure which, when it is heated and becomes gaseous, draws heat out of the refrigerator. The principal chemical used then was ammonia. But this is toxic and also volatile, and it made the manufacturing process prone to accidents. The manufacturers wanted a safe substitute.

Midgley worked on this problem for four years and developed an entirely new chemical compound for use as a coolant. It was a gas, chlorofluorocarbon, more commonly known as CFC. He demonstrated its virtues dramatically at a Chemical Society meeting in 1930. Ever the showman, he inhaled some CFC into his lungs, showing that it was non-toxic, and then blew out a candle with it, showing that it was non-inflammable.

Within a few years all refrigerators were made with CFC. Different CFCs were developed and other uses were found for them: in air conditioning units, as a propellant in aerosol sprays, in insulation and packaging, and as a solvent cleaner for electronic equipment.

We know now what happens to CFC. It drifts up into the stratosphere, where it eats away at the ozone layer that protects us from some of the ultraviolet (UV) radiation from the sun. Now the world is bathed in more ultraviolet radiation than it was before Midgley invented CFCs, 4 per cent more in Europe and North America, and more still in areas closer to the polar regions.

Thomas Midgley was something new in history. He changed the world in a way that no one had been able to do before the 20th century. He did not set out to do so. This was an unintentional by-product of his ingenuity and industry. He stands as the exemplar of modern humans, changing the planet with our new-found power and cleverness without setting out to do so.

(His death in 1945 was tragic, and yet one cannot help seeing in it an element of allegory. Stricken with polio and confined to his bed, he continued to work and, still inventive, devised an ingenious system of pulleys and harnesses that enabled him to get out of bed by himself. He became entangled in it and choked to death.)

For better or worse, whether we like it or not, we are all now, with our numbers and our powers and our inventions and the lifestyles we adopt, changing not merely our immediate surroundings, but the biosphere, the entire planet.

Life forms have not been passive passengers on Spaceship Earth. Over the long term, life has always changed the planet. Never more than in the first stages, some four billion years ago, when several chemicals somehow came together to form something with the ability to metabolize, that is, to absorb energy and use it to reproduce itself; in other words, life.

The earth then was much hotter than it is today, although the sun was weaker and gave out 25 per cent less heat. This requires some explanation. The reason, as scientists have worked out, is that the atmosphere was a mixture of carbon dioxide, methane and ammonia. These gases formed a blanket around the earth which trapped most of the heat from the sun, which would otherwise have been reflected out into space. It worked in the same way a greenhouse works: the glass allows the sun's rays to enter and warm the interior, and keeps some of the heat inside. The atmosphere was much like the atmosphere of Venus today; Venus is much hotter than earth and cannot sustain life. Today carbon dioxide and methane make up less than 0.1 per cent of the earth's atmosphere but they still play a part in creating a greenhouse effect.

Life began in the sea as single-celled organisms called cyano-bacteria, the algae that form as scum on the top of ponds, and these started immediately to change the planet and its climate. Algae and phytoplankton absorbed carbon dioxide from the rocks and broke it down into carbon and oxygen. Some of this oxygen became ozone and this created the ozone layer that provided a filter for ultraviolet radiation. Now life could form on land.

Plants came first, two billion years ago, and changed the atmos-phere by taking in carbon dioxide and exhaling oxygen. After a few hundred million years of plants, there was an atmosphere with enough oxygen for tiny animals to live in the sea. The great epic of animal life with the evolution of myriad varieties and the birth and death of species was under way.

The influence of living organisms on the planet led the British scientist James Lovelock in the 1970s to formulate the Gaia theory, which has been the subject of much attention. Named after the Greek earth goddess Gaia, it suggests that the earth functions as a living organism, regulating its atmosphere and its temperature to enable plant and animal life forms to survive. However, this theory leads to no comforting conclusion that the biosphere will sort out any problems we create. The Gaian earth may need life in some form, but it does not need us.

The planet was changing anyway over the aeons, due to chemical processes as well as biological ones. The continents moved about, heaving up mountain ranges and creating new seas, elements gave up some of themselves in radioactivity and gradually cooled, volcanoes brought hot sulphurous gases from underground and hurled them into the air, meteorites crashed into the Earth sending shock waves and dust clouds around the planet.

Life proliferated on land. After another billion years or so *Homo sapiens* came along. *Homo sapiens* was not as fast or as strong as some other animals but he developed his brain, and this made him more powerful than all the others. He learned to make tools, and to throw things, and to hunt in bands. He hunted some animals to extinction.

Ten to fifteen thousand years ago, people began to plant crops, which meant establishing communities and ownership of property. They turned landscapes into food resources, fields and open land into farms, and cleared forests. Occasionally this had disastrous results. Over-farming in the Middle East help turned some of what historians of the ancient world called the Fertile Crescent into desert. It is an educated guess that Mayans over-farmed the land in what is now Central America until the land gave out and most of them starved, dying in cities the ruins of which still contain their skeletons, several centuries before Columbus arrived in the New World.

As people travelled across the seas they took species with them, animals and plant seeds, sometimes on purpose, sometimes by accident. They took horses to the Americas, corn, tomatoes and potatoes to Europe, sugar cane to the Caribbean, rubber plants to Asia, dogs and rabbits to Australia. Today there is hardly a landscape in the world that has not been shaped partly by human activity.

Governments regulated to prevent environmental damage. In Tudor England and in Shogun Japan at about the same time, the governments passed laws restricting the cutting down of trees. Environmental damage does not respect national frontiers, and increasingly regulation has had to be international. The nations along the Rhine have combined to halt pollution of the river, the Mediterranean littoral countries have joined forces in an effort to clean up their sea, and Britain has agreed with other European countries to curb the sulphur emissions from its power stations and factories that were killing forests, as have the United States (US) and Canada. There are now more than 100 international environmental treaties in force.

People were slow to understand their power and the impact they can have. In 1909, the US Bureau of Lands said: 'The soil is the one indestructible, immutable asset that the nation possesses. It is the one resource that cannot be exhausted.' Twenty-five years later, events showed that the soil was far from indestructible. Over-farming in Midwestern states so weakened the topsoil that when drought dried it out and high winds came, it blew away as dust, turning farmland into the dust bowl and farming families into environmental refugees.

The first major human activities to affect not just one region but the entire planet were nuclear explosions. The full effect of these was realized in the 1950s, when what were then the three nuclear powers, the US, the Soviet Union and Britain, were carrying out nuclear bomb tests. At first, the death and destruction caused by the bombs on Hiroshima and Nagasaki were so appalling, so far beyond anything that weapons had achieved until that time, that there was little concern about tests. They did not blast or burn people to death so they were assumed to be harmless, just big bangs in the middle of nowhere. But scientists came to understand radioactive fallout. The test explosions contaminated particles with radioactivity and these particles rose to the upper atmosphere and drifted across the entire world. People everywhere received a minute dose of radiation. This raised by a statistically significant degree the number of cancer deaths all over the world.[3] It was an idea so new that it was difficult to grasp. When President Kennedy's science adviser explained radioactive strontium 90 to him, he pondered the matter, then looked out of the window at the drizzle coming down on to the White House lawn and asked, 'Do you mean that stuff's in the rain out there?'[4]

Scientists reported their findings to governments, and some made it their business to explain them to the public also. Public opinion was aroused. There was a special horror about radioactive pollution: it affects the genes, and so has the potential to damage generations yet unborn, far into the future. Even in the present generation, strontium 90, a radioactive isotope that does not exist in nature but is created by nuclear fission, settles in milk and in babies' bones. It seemed that the human race was now poisoning its own seed. This revelation had a powerful emotional impact.

The anti-bomb movement began as an anti-test movement. In America, a group of people took out a newspaper advertisement calling for a halt to tests saying: 'We must stop this contamination of the air, the milk people drink, the food we eat.' This was the beginning of SANE, the National Committee for a Sane Nuclear Policy, the principal American nuclear disarmament organization. In Britain the National Committee for the Abolition of Nuclear Weapons Tests became the Campaign for Nuclear Disarmament, CND, which brought 100,000 people out on marches to the nuclear weapons factory at Aldermaston and led to the biggest civil disobedience campaign since the suffragettes.

Non-governmental organizations put pressure on governments. These were not only mass protest movements but also organizations of scientists, including one, the Pugwash Movement, consisting of scientists on both sides of what was then the Iron Curtain. The US and the Soviet Union started negotiating on a treaty to ban nuclear weapons tests. The military establishments were worried that halting tests might mean falling behind in the arms race and negotiations became bogged down in technical details. Arguments about how to monitor the ban and how an underground nuclear test could be distinguished from an earthquake dragged on for years. Recondite scientific questions became politicized: about the likely number of earthquakes and the detection of tremors in different types of earth, about the effects of radioactivity. In 1963, the major powers agreed to a ban on tests in the atmosphere, which were what spread the radioactivity, and then to a ban on most underground tests.

The critical factors in this process were: the discovery of unforeseen and damaging effects; the role of scientists in explaining this to governments and disseminating information to the public; pressure from the public and non-governmental organizations; and the clash of concerns about the welfare of the human race with fears of national disadvantage. The success of the anti-nuclear movement gave rise to a new activism and a growth in the number and size of non-governmental organizations.

* * *

In the early 1970s, people learned that they were affecting the entire planet in another way, by damaging the ozone layer. This was a shock. The idea that we have this power, that if we don't tread carefully we can damage Mother Earth that nurtures us and sustains us, is a frightening one. It is the same kind of shock that, according to the child psychologist Jean Piaget, comes to a baby when it realizes that its mother is not an immutable and permanent presence but can be harmed or driven away temporarily by its actions.

This came at a time when environmental consciousness was growing. People struggled with community environmental issues: the pollution of rivers and streams, choking air in cities, the effects of pesticides on food and on our water, the disposal of garbage. There was a new realization of the extent to which human activities were taking over the natural world. Governments created departments of the environment with environment ministers.

The world had just experienced a growth in wealth unprecedented in history. Worldwide, gross national product, a rough guide to material wealth, more than doubled between 1950 and 1970. Food production had kept ahead of population. More people were hungry but many more people were eating better and living better than ever. Population was increasing at a faster pace than ever, from three billion in 1960 to six billion at the end of the second millennium. The rate of population growth has fallen since its peak in 1964 but the population is still growing.

In 1972 the Club of Rome published its milestone report *The Limits to Growth*, suggesting that we are coming up against the limits of the amount of materials that the planet can provide for its inhabitants and the amount of waste material it can absorb. The report was flawed, particularly in its forecasts of shortage of materials, but it was important in questioning seriously things that had been taken for granted: the desirability and feasibility of everyone becoming wealthier and acquiring more and more goods as people had done in the past.

Environmental concerns were given form at the first United Nations Conference on the Human Environment at Stockholm in 1972. The *Global 2000 Report,* produced by the US National Academy of Sciences for President Jimmy Carter, drew a picture of shortages and strains on global capacity. The Commission on Environment and Development headed by the Norwegian environment minister Gro Brundtland, an offshoot of the Stockholm Conference, proclaimed the goal of 'sustainable development', adding a new qualification to the universal goal of economic development. Figures were emerging constantly about dwindling resources: fish, forests, topsoil, water; and about the limited capacity of the atmosphere and the seas to take our detritus. The novel idea that the world might be living beyond its income gained ground.

The ozone layer issue, as it developed, contained the principal features of the nuclear test issue that were to figure in the climate change issue: the role of public opinion and of non-governmental organizations; new scientific discoveries leading the debate and changing its terms; the adoption of political/ideological positions; and consideration of consequences wider and further into the future than is usual in political matters.

Worry about the ozone layer concerned first of all the emissions from supersonic airliners. In the 1960s when the supersonic transport (SST) was on several companies' drawing boards, it was suggested that as they would be flying at a height of 9 miles, higher than other aircraft, the nitrous oxide from their exhausts would damage the ozone layer above the countries they were flying over and allow through more ultraviolet rays. The association of UV radiation with skin cancer was just becoming known. Partly because of these risks, US aircraft manufacturers abandoned their SST projects, wisely leaving it to the British and French governments to pioneer the new technology and spend money on Concorde that they will never recover. It was found that nitrous oxide made very little impact on the ozone layer.

The first suggestion that the chlorine in Thomas Midgley's CFCs was damaging the ozone layer came from two chemists at the University of California at Irvine, Mario Molina and Sherwood Rowland, who had become interested in CFCs and studied their properties. CFCs are stable compounds, which do not normally react with other chemicals, which is one reason they are useful. However, Molina and Rowland showed that when CFCs drift upwards into the stratosphere, the intense sunlight breaks off the chlorine atoms. Then each chlorine atom acts as a catalyst to the ozone, stripping away one oxygen atom from the three that make up an ozone molecule, so that what is left is no longer ozone. It then goes on to do the same to another ozone molecule.

At ground level, ozone, created out of normal oxygen by chemical pollutants, is harmful to the lungs. In the stratosphere it serves a benign function, shielding the earth from some of the sun's UV rays. It has this effect at ground level also: one reason for the high level of skin cancer in Australia and New Zealand is the absence of industrial pollution compared with European countries.

Molina and Rowland's report in 1974 in the scientific journal *Nature* was alarming. New uses for CFCs were being found all the time, and production had risen from 150,000 tonnes in 1960 to more than 800,000 in 1974. Only a small percentage of this was in domestic refrigerators. About a third was used in refrigeration, but most of this was in cold storage or industrial refrigeration, and half in aerosols. Their report said that because it takes a long time to decay, 90 per cent of the CFCs emitted into the atmosphere were still there, and would continue to erode the ozone layer for decades to come, up to 80 years. If they were right, a damaged ozone layer with more skin cancer cases would be a legacy we would leave to our children and grandchildren.

This was different from the issue of nuclear tests. Test nuclear explosions are carried out by governments in far-away places. But lots of people use hair sprays and furniture polish and refrigerators.

The US government and independent scientific institutes launched research projects. The subject is complicated. Ozone exists in only minute quantities in the atmosphere, and ozone molecules are constantly being created and destroyed by natural processes. There are several different kinds of CFCs, and other near-relations also damage the ozone layer: hydrochlorofluorocarbons, or HCFCs, which are used in some industrial refrigerants, and halons, which are used in fire extinguishers, and do not contain any chlorine but do contain bromine, which also attacks the ozone layer. They all differ in the strength of their effect on the ozone layer and also on the length of time over which this effect persists.

The US House of Representatives Environment Committee held hearings. The chemical industry, worried about its future as manufacturers of CFCs, weighed in with its opinion right away. RL McCarthy, a senior executive of DuPont, told the committee: 'The chlorine–ozone hypothesis is at this time purely speculative with no concrete evidence to support it'. Industrial corporations came together to form the Alliance for Responsible CFC Policy. They would argue against reductions in CFC use but they chose a title that did not sound negative.

Any reduction in the ozone shield would mean an increase in skin cancer and cataracts, and damage to crops. The World Health Organization (WHO) calculated that every 1 per cent reduction in the ozone layer means a 0.6 to 0.8 per cent increase in cataracts. It also said that increased UV radiation lowers resistance to infectious diseases. Like the cancer deaths caused by nuclear testing, the skin cancer cases and cataracts are statistical. A lot of people are going to get skin cancer anyway, and most of them will be people who spend a lot of time in the sun. The figure would be larger if the ozone layer were thinned out slightly, but no one could point to a particular case and say that CFC molecules were the cause.

The most serious damage is probably to the seas. An increase in UV radiation damages plankton, which upsets the ocean food chain and reduces the fish population. The United Nations Environment Programme (UNEP) found that phytoplankton are down 5 per cent in Antarctica, and one study showed that the population of

Adélie penguins has been reduced by 20 per cent because of the shortage of krill, their natural food, which is a result of the reduction in plankton.

There has already been an increase in skin cancer, particularly in southern latitudes, but this was probably due mostly to changes in attitudes and lifestyles. In the 19th century, pale, delicate skin was an attractive feature in men and women, implying also a purity of character. Now, when the dark forces of the id are let out and given their due, a tanned skin is admired in men and women both. A tan is classy and sexy. Men and women seek the sun on their holidays and lie in it, and more of them can afford to do so. Today the danger from UV rays is more widely recognized. People still seek a tan but some take precautions. In the sunshine land of Australia children are encouraged to wear hats and scarves outdoors, and the lifeguards who are one of the legendary attractions of Bondi beach keep their muscular torsos covered.

Environmentalists campaigned against the use of CFCs in aerosol spray cans. This was so effective in America that sales of aerosol products fell by two-thirds. Some manufacturers soon found substitute propellants and advertised on spray cans that they were CFC-free. In 1978 the US government banned the use of CFCs as propellants in aerosol cans, and the governments of Canada, Norway and Sweden followed suit. This was not difficult since alternative propellants were available. But this was not going to save the ozone layer if people in other countries continued to squirt CFCs into the air. Most European governments were reluctant to follow America's lead. The British government disputed the evidence of a serious threat to the ozone layer. In private, one official remarked dismissively that Americans are prone to over-react to health scares. European governments suspected America of trying to cripple trade rivals. Until 1974, the United States dominated the world market in CFCs as the major exporter, but from that year onwards European countries overtook it. The big chemical companies in Britain and Germany that manufactured CFCs had the ear of their governments and pressed this point. Nevertheless, the European Community agreed in 1980 to modest cuts in the use of CFCs, principally in aerosol sprays.

Pressed by Mostafa Tolba, the energetic Egyptian head of UNEP, the major governments set out to address the issue. The result was the Vienna Convention on the Protection of the Ozone Layer, signed in March 1985 by 20 countries, including all the major CFC-producing countries. This was a minimalist document. It said that the ozone layer might need protecting, but it did not mention CFCs. It committed the signatories to study the situation and take whatever measures were necessary.

However, a shock was to come. The British Antarctic Survey had been monitoring the atmosphere in Antarctica since 1957, when the programme was begun as part of Britain's contribution to the International Geophysical Year. In May 1985, two months after the signing of the Vienna Convention, Joe Farman, the scientist heading the team, reported in *Nature* that in the preceding ten years, the ozone layer over Antarctica had thinned in the summer months by 50 per cent, and in some places by even more. No one had imagined a reduction of the ozone layer on that scale. This hole in the ozone extended as far as New Zealand and the southern part of South America.

So unlikely did such a reduction in the ozone layer seem that US satellites which had been monitoring the ozone layer from 450 miles up had been programmed to record only small changes, since signs of a large change would be presumed to be mistakes. Bob Watson, the head of NASA's Upper Atmosphere Research Program, admitted that they had got it wrong: 'Scientists had become complacent. We thought we understood the processes', he said. Watson, a British-born chemist who has lost none of his English accent during his years in America, is a burly, bearded, often abrasive figure who was to play a big part in environmental repair from this time on. Having missed the hole in the ozone layer in the first instance he used his influence in Washington to press for action in this area. In 1999 he succeeded the Swedish scientist Bert Bolin as chairman of the Intergovernmental Panel on Climate Change.

It was still not certain that CFCs were to blame. But two years later, scientists gathered to examine the situation in Punta Arenas in southern Chile, the southernmost city in the world and the closest to the Antarctic continent. They analysed data brought back from the Antarctic stratosphere by a U2 plane loaded with scientific detection equipment. This nailed CFCs as the culprit; they found that the ice crystals in the clouds speed up the process by which they shed their chlorine atoms.

Yet even now there was still no unequivocal finding of a worldwide danger. The chemistry of the upper atmosphere and the patterns of the world weather system were not fully understood, nor are they today. The phenomenon in Antarctica could have been an anomaly. There is a seasonal variation in ozone levels. Nor was it certain how much more UV radiation was actually reaching the earth. Curiously, there was no agreed methodology for measuring it and no reliable worldwide records. In 1986, NASA reported that a study of different models and measurements 'reveals several disturbing detailed disagreements . . . that limit our confidence in the predictive capability of these models'.

As with many other environmental issues, much of the discussion was an argument between alarmist exaggeration and defensive complacency. The alarmists said that one consequence already was a rash of cataracts among sheep in Patagonia, and blind fish. No one has found the blind fish and the cataracts among sheep were due to the spread of a fungal infection. Also, as with other environmental issues, industry exaggerated the costs of dealing with the problem. DuPont, a major CFC producer, said $385 billion worth of capital equipment worldwide was dependent on CFCs. The automobile industry said it would cost $1500 to recharge a car's air conditioning unit with a substitute for CFCs. The cost today is between $200 and $800.

The argument became an ideological dispute, as most environmental problems do at some point. This has emotional logic. Someone who feels largely content with the prevailing economic system and the way society is run is likely to resist the idea that it can have disastrous consequences and that measures must be taken to rectify these. Someone who worries about a system that encourages acquisitiveness and creates inequality will probably be more ready to accept that there is and perhaps even should be a price to pay. Many conservatives regard environmentalists as simply anti-growth and anti-capitalist – 'watermelons', green on the outside and red on the inside. (This identification of environmentalism with the Left is not inevitable. Conservation is conservative; some rural environmentalists are simply defending their traditional way of life, and in the 1930s the most environmentally conscious government in Europe, in its wildlife protection measures as well as its rhetorical respect for nature, was the government of Nazi Germany.)

Not surprisingly, there was opposition to action on the ozone layer among members of the Reagan Administration, temperamentally opposed to government regulation, even more opposed to international regulation, and suspicious of alarm calls about the environment. Washington officials tried to change the Administration's position on the Vienna Convention at the last moment, and only some furious arguing on the transatlantic telephone by Assistant Secretary of State James Malone, who headed the US delegation in Vienna, ensured that America would sign up.[5] Secretary of the Interior Donald Hodel said the answer to the problem was not regulation but wide-brimmed hats and sun-tan oil, not government regulation but good old self-reliance.

Even as the science advanced, a few people held out. When Rowland and Molina along with a Dutch scientist were awarded the Nobel Prize in Chemistry for their findings about the ozone layer, in 1995, Fred Singer, one of the few scientists to remain sceptical, said the award was 'politically motivated'.

* * *

Government officials met to agree to cut down or even ban the use of CFCs. At first it was hard going. They disagreed on what chemicals should be included, whether it would be an outright freeze or a gradual reduction, and what form the controls should take. America continued to press for stronger measures. Most Europeans wanted to hold back, although now the German government switched its stance and came out for a ban. A Soviet official summoned up a dramatic picture of the Hermitage Museum in Leningrad with its art treasures burning down and fire-fighters standing by helplessly because of the ban on halon. Some argued that the science was still uncertain.

UNEP's Mostafa Tolba decided to give the process a fillip. Atmosphere scientists were meeting at a conference in Wurzburg, Germany in April 1987. Tolba asked five groups from five different countries to bring their forecasts on the ozone layer to a special meeting. When they assembled they found the conference room had been double-booked so they crowded into Bob Watson's hotel room. Sitting on chairs, on his bed and on the floor they compared forecasts, and all agreed that the damage to the ozone layer was serious, and passed on their findings to the conference.

It was, and is, difficult for government officials, accustomed to work for what traditionally forms the national interest, to come to grips with this issue. Richard Benedick, the chief American delegate to conferences on the ozone layer, reflected later on the unique situation: 'Military strength was irrelevant. Economic power was not decisive. Neither great wealth nor sophisticated technology was necessary to produce large quantities of ozone-destroying chemicals. Traditional notions of national sovereignty became questionable when local decisions and activities could affect the well-being of the entire planet.'[6]

In discussion of the issue, the 'dilemma of the global commons' is often raised; this is a phrase coined by the writer Garrett Hardin in a widely noted article *The Tragedy of the Commons*. The 'commons' means what it has meant historically, grazing land common to a rural farming community. The global commons are, analogously, those parts of the globe that are held in common by all the inhabitants, such as the atmosphere, the oceans, the sea bed. As Hardin sees it,[7] the tragedy of the commons is that it is in each individual's interest to put as many of his animals as he can on the common. But if everyone does this, the result will be over-grazing and everyone will suffer: 'Each man is locked into a system that compels him to increase his herd without limit, in a world that is limited. Ruin is the destination to which all men rush in a society that believes in the freedom of the commons.'

But it is not really a dilemma, unlike the prisoners' dilemma, a situation often depicted for learning purposes in international relations theory. In this, each of a pair of prisoners, separated from the other, is under pressure to act selfishly to the detriment of both, because he does not know how the other will act.[8] In the commons situation everyone knows what everyone else is doing so there is a simple answer – simple in conception, not in execution – and that is cooperation and joint restraint. That was in fact what was usually practised on grazing commons in past times, either formally, adhering to a set of written rules, or tacitly.

The nations have reached agreement in the recent past on husbanding parts of the global commons, but only where it does not cost much. There is a set of international agreements on sharing out the electromagnetic spectrum for communications purposes. There are international agreements to keep certain activities from outer space. Agreements on managing other global commons, such as Antarctica, have been achieved, albeit with difficulty.

The concept of the commons has now been established in international law and customs, and with it other new concepts. The Law of the Sea Treaty states that the ocean floor and anything found on it are the 'common heritage of Mankind'. This term had previously been applied to cultural artefacts, such as the Angkor Wat temple in Cambodia and Abu Simbel in Egypt, which was moved up the Nile through a huge international effort to save it from flooding when the Aswan Dam was built. Another new concept is enshrined in the Antarctic Treaty. The area is to be preserved for its 'wilderness value'. This is saying that there is value in preserving a part of the globe in something close to its pristine state.

Spurred on by the new findings, government officials negotiated a treaty, termed a protocol, to be signed in Montreal in September 1987. Richard Benedick, the chief American negotiator, admitted that there was a degree of uncertainty, but argued that, given the dangers, it was important to act without waiting for complete certainty. 'If we are to err in designing measures to protect the ozone layer, then let us, conscious of our responsibility to future generations, err on the side of caution', he said.

Until now, the developing world, as the poorer countries of the world were now called, had shown little interest in the issue. They were neither major producers nor consumers of CFCs. Furthermore, UV radiation discriminates racially. It affects white people much more than people with darker skins. A Malaysian scientist even worried that South Asians had neglected the issue complacently despite the fact that they get more of the sun's rays: 'Because people living in the high dosage belt have a darker skin tan which provides greater protection to the skin against ultraviolet radiation, this high UV radiation situation has not been considered seriously.'[9]

Now these countries stepped in. Their principal concern was not the effects of ozone layer depletion but the effect of a ban on CFCs. Although they were minor consumers of CFCs now they wanted the good things that are made with CFCs in the future. Why should Asians and Africans not also have refrigerators in their homes? Why should they not enjoy frozen food? The protocol had to take this into account. Only a few developing countries were represented at Vienna but half the 60 countries represented at the Montreal negotiations were from the developing world.

The Montreal Protocol as finally agreed laid down a schedule for cutting production and use of CFCs, HCFCs and halons. Different chemicals involved were assigned figures corresponding to an ozone depleting potential, or ODP. CFC 11 and 12, the most common, were given an ODP of 1. Others ranged from 0.6 to 10. The protocol took 1986 production levels as its benchmark and ruled that each country must peg production and consumption of CFCs at the 1986 level of ODP by 1989, 20 per cent below it by 1993, and 50 per cent below it by 1996. A country could choose the mix to achieve this. Halon ODP was to be pegged at 1986 levels by 1992. CFCs already in use could be recycled. There are concessions to meet special needs. Countries with small CFC industries

had a special allowance to trade. The Soviet Union had a dispensa-
tion to continue with production plants that were already planned.
Developing world countries could delay their production cut-backs.

The treaty provides a penalty for staying out and an incentive
to join in. Trade in CFCs and CFC products is not allowed between
countries that are within the protocol and those outside. So once
the industrial countries have signed, a developing country outside
the protocol cannot get CFCs or CFC products, one reason for
not staying out. The carrot to match this stick was the setting up
of an Interim Fund to help developing world countries to adapt
production to using substitutes for CFCs.

In Washington, White House chief of staff John Sununu pre-
vailed on the Administration to refuse at first to contribute to the
Interim Fund, to the dismay of other signatories. Sununu, a former
engineer, had strong reservations about all claims of danger to the
global environment. Budget director Richard Darman shared his
view, and talked in a speech about 'anti-growth, command-and-
control, centralistic environmentalism'. But under pressure from
within and from Congress, the Administration reversed this stand
and supported the convention.

The ratification procedure was unusual. The protocol would
come into force when the convention was ratified, not by a fixed
number of the signatories, but by 11 countries which together
accounted for 90 per cent of consumption of CFCs and halons.
In effect this meant it had to be ratified by the US and four
other major industrial countries. The battle was joined in the US
Administration and Senate.

The Montreal Protocol was seen to be inadequate even before
the ink was dry. In March 1988, an international panel of scientists
concluded that the ozone layer had been reduced, not just over
Antarctica but over the northern hemisphere also, by up to 6 per

cent in the winter months, depending on the latitude, and 3 per cent in the summer months. Europe and North America were getting more UV radiation. The negotiators of the Montreal Protocol had assumed that the ozone layer would be reduced worldwide by an average of 2 per cent by the middle of the 21st century. Now it seemed that this had happened already.

American industry accepted what it saw as the inevitable and switched sides. The Alliance for Responsible CFC Policy lived up to its title and came out in support of international regulation.

More important, industry everywhere looked for substitutes for CFCs. As one chemist working for ICI in Britain said, 'We trawled the molecules, looking for one that had the right properties, one that had a very low boiling point, that was not flammable, that can flow, and was not too costly.' ICI and DuPont in America turned to hydrofluorocarbons (HFCs), containing no chlorine, as a substitute refrigerant. In America, AT&T announced that it had a substitute for CFC 113, which is used as a solvent in the electronics industry, and this made Japan more ready to sign up for a ban. Chemical industries from several countries joined forces to develop substitutes for halons in fire-fighting equipment. The US Environmental Protection Agency and two private institutes sponsored a trade fair devoted to alternatives to CFCs in Washington in January 1988.

By this time another man-made global environmental problem had appeared: it seemed that we were changing the climate. This became linked in the public consciousness with the ozone layer issue. The two issues are also linked scientifically. CFCs contribute to global warming by letting more sunlight through. They also contribute to global warming in another way that illustrates the complexity and interconnectedness of living things and the planet.

Ultraviolet radiation reduces the ability of algae to photosynthesize, and so reduces the amount of carbon dioxide taken out of the air. They were also linked politically. Positions taken up in respect of the ozone layer could, and usually were, transferred to the larger issue of climate change.

The British government swung behind the ozone issue and with the support of UNEP, it convened a Conference on Saving the Ozone Layer in September 1988. This had two aims: speeding up the process begun at Montreal, and bringing in more of the poorer countries. It succeeded in its first aim. On the eve of the conference, the United States and the European Community both announced that they would phase out CFCs by the end of the century. It was less successful with the other. Major developing world countries raised new objections. They saw now some of the ways that the producers of CFCs could manipulate the situation. But they also saw that they had some leverage. Now at last the West needed something from them and they could give it or withhold it.

The Chinese representative said that the Interim Fund for the transfer of CFC-free technology was not enough and proposed a new and more generous mechanism. The Indian environment minister, Ziul Rahman Ansari, supported the idea and pointed out that almost all the CFC in the atmosphere had been put there by the wealthy nations: 'Lest someone think of this fund as charity, I would like to remind them of the excellent principle "the polluter pays" adopted in the developed world', he said.

Without the accession of China and India, the two most populous countries in the world, any treaty to limit CFCs would be nullified as these countries developed and provided their people with refrigerators. To keep developing countries on board, more dispensations were given to them as the schedule of phasing out CFCs was revised.

Scientific findings set the pace. William Reilly, the director of the US Environmental Protection Agency, said the London targets 'may prove to be inadequate', and he was right. Every year brought news that the depletion of the ozone layer was greater than had been thought. The targets for reduction were ratcheted upwards at one meeting after another as more was discovered about the thinning of the ozone layer.

At the first meeting of the parties of the Montreal Convention, in April 1989 in Helsinki, delegates agreed to aim at phasing out CFCs by the end of the century. In 1991 measurements showed that the thinned-out area in the ozone layer was still spreading. Ozone levels in the winter and early spring had been reduced by up to 5 per cent in the last decade. The US Environmental Protection Agency calculated that this would cause 12 million additional cases of skin cancer over the next 50 years and 200,000 deaths. The following year the parties met in Copenhagen and agreed that industrialized countries would phase out CFCs by 1996.

CFCs and most halons were officially phased out in the Western world in 1996. They are still being produced in the developing world albeit in reduced quantities, and will be around until 2010. HCFC production has been cut but will not be phased out until 2030. Some halons are allowed for what are deemed essential services: the US Federal Aviation Authority insists that all passenger aircraft have fire extinguishers with halon on board. China, India and Mexico have increased their production of CFC 12, which they still use in refrigeration, as they are allowed to under the Convention. Also, a lot of it leaks from old refrigeration systems, even though this could be destroyed chemically.

A flourishing black market in CFCs has developed. Thousands of tonnes are smuggled across borders, sometimes disguised as other products. Russia is allowed to use recycled CFCs, but it exports more supposedly recycled CFCs than it has facilities to recycle. Mexico is allowed to manufacture some CFCs which are smuggled across the border into America. Customs officials in Miami say CFCs are second only to cocaine as a smugglers' import. German police cracked a smuggling ring in July 1998 that had already distributed 800 tonnes of Chinese-made CFCs around Europe.

CFCs are used mostly in small industries. The person who comes to service the cold air unit in the beer cellar in a British pub, or the automobile workshop in America that services a car's air conditioning unit, may well be using illicit CFCs, perhaps without knowing it. (It must also be said, as American drivers know on hot summer days, that air conditioning units using HFCs are not so efficient at cooling.)

This is also a factor in the problem of managing the planet. We now have major governments in what political scientists call weak states, in which the state structure is not strong enough to ensure or even to make it likely that laws are obeyed. The governments, whatever agreements they sign, cannot ensure that their citizens stick to the rules. The problem of compliance, like the issues at stake, transcends national borders.

CFC smuggling joins the list of environmental crimes. This seems inevitable. Once there are rules, it is usually profitable for someone to break them. So smugglers break the law to sell rhino horn and banned ivory, and other groups transport toxic waste in violation of international agreements.

At the end of 1998, the World Meteorological Organization reported that the amount of CFC in the atmosphere is coming down and the ozone layer is repairing itself. However scientists have confirmed that global atmospheric warming is delaying this process in a way which shows the complex and sometimes unexpected interactions of planetary processes.

The increase in carbon in the atmosphere, which has made the Arctic regions warmer in recent years, has made the stratosphere in the Arctic, which is where the ozone layer is colder. Scientists have confirmed what many suspected: that the ozone layer is sensitive to temperature, and that a lower temperature means a reduced ozone layer. So now that we are phasing out CFCs, which have damaged the ozone layer, global warming is delaying its recovery.

This will, in any case, be a slow process. As Joe Farman told a BBC interviewer: 'For 15 years, you put the wrong thing into the atmosphere and you end up with something that takes 100 years to put right.' Nonetheless, as with nuclear testing, we recognized one way in which we were damaging the planetary environment and have stopped doing so.

The questions raised by the ozone issue are a pointer to the questions raised on an even larger scale by the climate change issue, and so are the methods of dealing with the problem. Many of the characteristics of the ozone layer agreement are new to international relations. They are characteristics also of the climate change agreements because they answer the same needs: the acceptance of different responsibilities among the rich and poor nations; the transfer of resources to poorer nations so that they can play their part; the treaty in the form of a convention, which allows new targets to be slotted in as the situation changes and our scientific knowledge increases; the long time-scale of measures and results. They are likely also to be characteristics of other agreements on the planetary environments.

CHAPTER 2

THE CLIMATE
OF THE TIMES

*Where environmental issues differ from the subject matter of traditional
security studies is not in the absence of threats but in the absence of
enemies. They are threats without enemies* – Gwyn Prins[1]

WHEN THE WEATHER is different, the world
is different. Twenty thousand years ago, during the last Ice Age, ice
sheets covered most of Europe and North America and sea levels
were 100 metres lower than they are today. Britain was joined to
the European continent, Alaska and Siberia were joined by a land
bridge across what are now the Bering Straits, and Australia was
joined to what is now the Indonesian archipelago. Sixty thousand
years ago, when the world was warmer than it is now, sea levels
were 16 feet higher and the Sahara was lush and green.

The earth has undergone periodic ice ages, due to changes in
the tilt of the planet relative to its orbit around the sun and in the
orbit itself. If the earth follows the pattern of past climatic change,
another ice age can be expected 60,000 years from now.

Other factors affect the weather. Changes in vegetation alter
the amount of sunlight reflected and hence the temperature.

Occasionally a volcanic eruption will throw up so much dust that it circles the world, blotting out sunshine and creating a cooler climate for several months. The eruption at Tambor in Indonesia in 1815 produced what a diarist in New England called 'the year without a summer'; the volcanic explosion on Krakatoa in 1883 produced cooling and magnificent sulphur-laden sunsets around the world for three years; and in 1992 the Mount Pinatubo eruption in the Philippines created a dip in the global warming trend.

Five million years ago, when the climate in Africa became drier and the rain forests shrank, life became difficult for the apes who lived in the trees. One kind of ape responded by coming down from the trees and learning to walk upright and live in the grasslands of the savanna. Its upright posture gave it two advantages: it gave it the free use of its hands; and it exposed less of its body to sunlight and also kept it further from the warm ground, so that it cooled more easily. This upright primate became *Homo sapiens* and learned to adapt to the weather. From East Africa he spread across the world. Unlike most other species of mammal, *Homo sapiens* lives in many different climates, from the tropics to the far north.

Civilization began with a change in the climate. When the last Ice Age ended and temperatures around the world rose to about their present level, our ancestors began to cultivate land and live in settled communities.

The world's climate has changed in historic times for reasons that scientists still do not understand. There was a Medieval warm period, from the 11th to the 14th century, when the temperature seems to have been higher than in the preceding centuries, and a period known as the 'little Ice Age' from the 16th to the 18th century.

We have evidence of the warmer period in northern Europe from economic and social history. Vineyards flourished in England in those years, people farmed 200 feet higher in the Alps than they do today, and the Vikings colonized, and named, Greenland. (The naming may have been partly for propaganda reasons; the first Vikings to arrive wanted to encourage others to follow and settle there.) Floodwaters enroached on low-lying areas of The Netherlands so that inhabitable parts of the country became smaller.

At the end of this period, in the early 1300s, when the weather became colder, records tell of famines in northern Europe, Greenland became the largely ice-covered land it is today, and the descendants of the Viking settlers perished.

There is also historic evidence of colder temperatures from the 16th century up to the mid-19th century. During the American War of Independence, the British garrison in New York hauled cannon across the ice from Staten Island to Manhattan. Today the ice in New York harbour is not thick enough to walk on in even the coldest weather. It is commonplace to point to accounts of ice fairs on the River Thames at London at which revellers roasted oxen.

It is usually said that the world was 1 degree centigrade warmer during the Medieval warm period and a degree colder in the 'little Ice Age', but there is less certainty about these figures than most writers on the subject acknowledge. The largest body of scientists ever to study the climate, the Intergovernmental Panel on Climate Change (IPCC), speak of 'an incoherent picture' and 'contradictory records', and says of temperatures over the last thousand years: 'The records are still too sparse to provide a complete global analysis, and must in general be interpreted in a regional context.' It goes on: 'At this point it is . . . not possible to conclude that global temperatures in the Medieval warm period were comparable to the warm decades of the late Twentieth Century.'[2]

One lesson from this is the amazingly large changes brought about by a small change in global average temperature. If the temperature in the room in which you are sitting rose or fell by 1 degree centigrade, you would barely notice it.

Changes in climate have been a factor in history. We have to stretch our imaginations to appreciate how direct and vital a part the climate has played in people's lives and, inevitably, in history. Most of us in the West live largely insulated from the weather, in buildings and even vehicles which are heated and air conditioned. We are remote from the production of the food we eat. Our pattern of working and sleeping is largely independent of natural cycles since much of the light we live by is electric. The modern city-dweller never sees the real darkness of night. But for almost all of history, people have lived their lives very differently, exposed to the climate and subject to its vagaries. Most people have always been engaged in raising food (in Western countries most people until the present century) which means they were affected powerfully by even slight changes.

One cannot say with confidence exactly how climate has affected the course of history; historical events rarely have one cause. One can, however, identify a coincidence of climatic change and other events. In the 4th century BC, when records indicate warmer weather in the Mediterranean area, farming became easier in the Roman lands and the republic prospered; the snows in the Alpine passes melted and the legions marched through them to begin the Roman expansion across Europe. Some historians identify colder climate in the 5th century AD and consequent agricultural deficiencies with the decline of the Roman Empire and the invasions from the north. The French Revolution followed two years of unaccustomed bad weather and consequent poor harvests.

In the 20th century, a change in the weather altered the course of history. In the summer of 1941 the German government's weather service under Franz Baur forecast a mild winter in eastern Europe arriving late, and on this basis Hitler ordered the invasion of Russia to begin in June. He counted on a quick blitzkrieg for victory to match those in the West, for the German economy was not organized for a long war. His forces swept ahead in the first months and reached the outskirts of Moscow, but then came early frost and the coldest winter in a half-century; the German war machine ground to an agonizing halt in the snow, and Nazi Germany's long road to defeat began.

Now the world's weather is changing, apparently under the impact of some of the gases that we are emitting. Every week brings more evidence of this change. The World Meteorological Organization (WMO) reported that global temperatures throughout the world in 1998 were the highest since records began 150 years ago, that every year in the last 20 the temperature was higher than the long-term average over the last century, and that seven of the ten warmest years on record have been in the 1990s. Temperature graphs show a steady rise amounting to at least 1 degree centigrade since the 1960s. All the indications are that we will soon undergo a greater change in temperature than we have seen since the last Ice Age.

The US National Climate Data Center says the American climate has become more extreme in the last 15 years with more conditions outside the normal range of variability. This was borne out by two photographs printed in the *New York Times* in the same week in November 1998. One showed tourists battling through a snowstorm in normally sunny Las Vegas; the other showed, even more freakishly for a New York winter, sun-bathers on Orchard Beach in the Bronx basking in 23-degree centigrade heat. The 1993 floods in the Midwest were the worst that the region has ever experienced, and the Oklahoma City tornado in May 1999 had the strongest winds ever recorded in America. In Britain's West Country, floods expected once in every century are occurring every two or three years.

As government officials met to discuss climate change in Geneva, Alpine glaciers a few dozen miles away that had been stable for

10,000 years were shrinking, in some cases bringing rock falls on villages. The 1995 World Skiing Championships due to be held in the Sierra Nevada Mountains in Spain were cancelled because there was not enough snow. El Niño swept across the world more powerfully than ever before causing devastation. Central America was hit by the most devastating hurricane in its recorded history.

Some of the predicted health effects are also being seen already. The World Health Organization reports a 'qualitative leap' in malaria cases associated with extreme weather conditions, an increase in Rift Valley fever, another mosquito-borne disease, in Kenya, and cholera in Latin America. Medical authorities warned of new mosquito-borne diseases in southern England and New York. The city of New Orleans reported a plague of cockroaches and termites due to the absence of frost in five successive years. The changing weather is now the stuff of newspaper reports almost daily. Several cities have experienced record-breaking heat waves: New York, Chicago, Moscow and Delhi. In London the warmer summers have meant that the predominantly clay soil is cracking, and insurance companies report an unprecedented number of claims for house subsidence.

The change has been different in different places, the warming most marked nearer to the polar regions. In Alaska and northern Canada, and much of Siberia also, the average temperature has risen by more than 3 degrees centigrade in the last 30 years. In Alaska, the melting of the permafrost is signalled by tilting houses and falling telegraph poles as the frozen ground thaws, and clumps of trees sinking into what have become swamps. Cruise ships used to sail up to the Columbia Glacier so that passengers could look at its white wall; the glacier has retreated 8 miles in the last 15 years and can barely be seen from the sea.

The Arctic ice cap is thinning. Studies carried out by the US Navy, which has had submarines sailing under the Arctic ice for many years, show that the cap has become up to 40 per cent thinner in some places in recent times. The Scott Polar Institute in Cambridge says that the area of Arctic ice has been shrinking since the 1970s.

In the Weddell Sea in Antarctica, where Ernest Shackleton's ship was crushed by the ice, the temperature has risen by 2.5 degrees centigrade. In November 1994 the Argentine Antarctic Institute predicted that a large part of the Larsen Ice Cap would break away within ten years. A piece 48 miles long and 22 miles wide broke off four months later. Julian Paren of the British Antarctic Survey cites some images of the changing continent that linger in his mind: 'Armadas of icebergs leaving ice-free conditions in their wake; penguins migrating as their preferred ice ocean domain slips away; a lonely plant, the first coloniser of an increasingly hospitable Antarctic island; the view from a helicopter flying through gaping fissures in the ice shelves.'[3]

The melting of Arctic ice and Antarctic ice shelves will not raise sea levels since they float on the surface already and so displace their own weight in water. However, this does not mean that it will have no effect. The earth's weather system is connected to ocean currents and temperatures, and the melting ice can produce far-reaching changes. Scientists are watching Antarctica as a harbinger of what is happening the planet. Gene Domack, an earth scientist from Hamilton College in Clinton, New York who took part in a recent expedition to Antarctica, explains: 'It could turn out to be the canary in the mine. If the canary goes, you have to be worried.'[4]

It is not all bad. In British cities people are spending more time in their gardens, and outdoor cafés and restaurants are proliferating. A look at temperatures in central London shows that between

1964 and 1969, the average temperature in July was 15.4 degrees centigrade, and between 1994 and 1999 it was 17.2 degrees centigrade. (In 1774–79 it was 14.8 degrees centigrade according to Meteorological Office records.) Spring arrives earlier, in America by eight days above the 45th parallel, a line that passes through Maine, Minnesota and Oregon. Many farmers have a growing period a week longer, and plants are taller and leafier. But the plants may produce fewer nutrients, and in the longer term pests and water shortage will probably cut back harvests.

For most people, the change will bring discomfort or worse, in many cases much worse. The International Red Cross reported in June 1999 that natural disasters in the previous year were in aggregate the worst on record, and for the first time more refugees were fleeing environmental damage than war. International Red Cross president Astrid Heiberg said: 'Everyone is aware of the environmental problems of global warming and deforestation on the one hand and the social problems of poverty and growing shanty towns on the other. When these two factors collide, you have a new scale of catastrophe.'

* * *

The first man to suggest that pumping carbon dioxide into the atmosphere would cause the climate to change was the Swedish chemist and Nobel laureate Svante Arrhenius. He published a paper in 1896 forecasting that increasing the carbon content in the atmosphere would enhance the greenhouse effect. This is the process by which a blanket of gas traps some of the heat that comes in with the sun's rays. Arrhenius said that doubling the carbon content in the atmosphere would increase the temperature by between 4 and 6 degrees centigrade. This figure is remarkably close to today's findings.

In 1957, when scientists around the world came together for the International Geophysical Year, David Keeling of the Scripps Institution of Oceanography in San Diego revived the idea, and suggested that it would be wise to monitor the build-up of carbon dioxide in the atmosphere. Roger Revelle, a leading oceanographer, set up a monitoring station on top of Mauna Loa, an 11,000-foot-high mountain in Hawaii, far away from industrial smoke. The Mauna Loa record since then shows a steady increase of just under 0.5 per cent a year. The rising graph has a geometric regularity, with one peak and one trough each year. Other observatories around the world began taking similar measurements and their findings were in agreement.

Revelle immediately saw the implications of this, and began talking up the greenhouse effect, as he and a few others began to call it, to classes he taught at Harvard University on population. One of his more attentive pupils was Al Gore. To young Gore, the idea that humans could change the weather was a startlingly new one. He began reading about it, and became seized with the idea that the changing of the environment was the most important thing happening in the world. Twelve years later, as a freshman Congressman, he got Revelle to testify before the first congressional hearings on climate change.

Back then, not many people were paying attention. At the United Nations (UN) Conference on the Environment in Stockholm in 1972, the biggest meeting on environmental matters that had ever taken place, climate change was barely mentioned. But in 1979 the United Nations Environment Programme (UNEP) and the World Meteorological Organization organized the first World Climate Conference in Geneva. The assembled scientists decided that the theory of climate change due to the greenhouse effect was plausible, although not proven, and the question was now on the international agenda. Follow-up meetings were held, and at each, scientists took a more serious view of the build-up of carbon. Climate modelling indicated that greenhouse gas 'forcing' – meaning adding greenhouse gases to the atmosphere – should make the world warmer, and with the increase of greenhouse gases it appeared to be getting warmer. But they were cautious about committing themselves on man-made climate change.

Scientists have several sources of evidence about the past climate. Records going back to the Pharaohs, and diaries and letters tell us something about conditions. Measuring tree rings on long-lived trees also provides evidence. Each ring denotes a successive year, and the thickness and consistency varies with soil moisture. Pushing the time horizon back further, palaeoclimatology, the study of climate in prehistoric times, is a developing science. (It is not all that new: *Webster's Dictionary* dates the word back to 1903.) Here the sources of evidence are fewer and require greater ingenuity. Fossils of certain plants which grow only within a narrow climate belt give clues, and even fossils of insects and bacteria. The carbon 14 test, which can tell by radioactive decay the time when an organism was alive, is a contribution of physics. Chemical analysis of rocks can also yield information.

Scientists have found new evidence by digging down in the ice cap covering Greenland and, at the other end of the world, the ice cap in Antarctica. The ice caps are several thousand feet thick. Each year a little snow falls here. The snow is compressed into ice and air bubbles remain in this ice. The next year more snow falls on top and this ice is forced downward. Scientists pull out ice through a long thin tube, and date it by its depth. Analysis of the air bubbles in a layer of ice and of the relative quantity of two isotopes of oxygen can tell us the temperature at the surface at the time the ice was formed. Russian scientists in Antarctica have dug deepest, more than a mile down, to examine ice than was formed when snow fell 200,000 years ago. Analysis of the ice layers show a close correlation between carbon dioxide concentration and temperature, the two rising and falling together.

Recently, British scientists have found a link between CO_2 and climate which goes back much further, and which indicates that the greenhouse effect at one time killed a lot of the plant life on earth, and animals as well. A team from Sheffield University looked at fossils of leaves dating back 206 million years from Sweden and Greenland and examined the stomata, tiny openings that let in carbon dioxide. The date is significant because it was at the time of the Triassic extinction, one of five short periods during which most of life on earth was wiped out for reasons that scientists do not yet understand. They found that the density of stomata on the leaves dropped, and since this happens in response to changing levels of carbon dioxide, they were able to estimate that carbon dioxide levels rose, from 600 parts per million to 2400 parts per million.

Dr Jenny McElwain, who headed the team, explains: 'There were a lot of volcanic eruptions of the basalt kind. These do not produce great clouds of dust but they do produce carbon. Modelling of the greenhouse effect indicates that putting this amount of carbon into the atmosphere would have raised temperatures by four or five degrees. Leaf fossils confirmed that this is what happened. The leaves that survived were smaller ones, which could dissipate the extra heat. We think the heat is what killed off most of the plants.'

Presumably, animals died either because of the heat or because the plants on which they depended for food died, although Dr McElwain, being cautious, says they have no direct data on this.

In June 1988, the US Senate's Energy and Natural Resources Committee held hearings into the question of whether man-made carbon emissions were causing temperature change. As it turned out, they were timely, because America was in the grip of the hottest heat wave and the worst drought in decades. Midwest farmland was drying up for lack of irrigation water, thousands of farmers were on the edge of bankruptcy, and outside in the Washington streets the pavements were baking in 38-degree-centigrade heat. The press and the public were interested in climate.

The headlines were made by James Hansen, the director of the Goddard Space Studies Center at NASA, the National Aeronautics and Space Administration. 'The evidence is pretty strong that the greenhouse effect is here', he told the committee. 'I'm 99 per cent certain that current temperatures reflect a warming trend'. No scientist had ever come out so positively before on the subject.

The Canadian government called a conference on climate change in Toronto in September 1988. The climatologist Stephen Schneider of the National Center for Atmospheric Research in Boulder, Colorado, a prominent figure in this and other climate change meetings, called this conference 'the Woodstock of the greenhouse effect'. There is indeed a parallel, for it was a feelgood festival of concern and consciousness-raising – the 1960s language seems appropriate – reaching conclusions that were more visionary than practical. The assembled scientists concluded unequivocally that emissions of carbon and some other gases enhanced the greenhouse effect and were warming the atmosphere dangerously. They declared: 'Humanity is conducting an enormous experiment with the planet, whose ultimate consequences could be second only to a global nuclear war'. They called for a 20 per cent reduction in carbon dioxide emissions by 2005, which came to be known as the Toronto target. Ultimately, they wanted the world to reduce emissions by 50 per cent.

The greenhouse effect created by our atmosphere is necessary for life as we know it. Without it our planet would be colder than in any ice age. The gases that we are putting into the atmosphere do not create the greenhouse effect but enhance it. Carbon dioxide is the principal one. It exists in the atmosphere in very small quantities. It is produced by most industrial activities, but particularly by burning fossil fuels.

When we burn coal or oil, we are releasing carbon that has been sequestered for hundreds of thousands of years. In the atmosphere, the carbon combines with oxygen to make carbon dioxide. Coal produces the most carbon, oil is next and natural gas less – about a third as much as coal per unit of useful energy.

The amount of CO_2 in the atmosphere has gone up by about 30 per cent since the start of the Industrial Revolution (that is, 1750) and it is now 365 parts per million. This may not seem like a lot, but it has a powerful effect. Sulphur dioxide is the principal urban pollutant, and at its highest concentration, when it can be seen in the smog and even smelled, it is only 200 parts per *billion*. Like the ozone-depleting CFCs, CO_2 lingers in the atmosphere for anywhere from 50 to 200 years.

Growing plants, and particularly trees, because of their size, take in carbon dioxide from the atmosphere. Humans have cut down 45 per cent of the trees that once covered the earth to make room for their activities, including agriculture. This has accounted for about 15 per cent of the increase in CO_2. On average, cutting down an acre of growing trees adds between 100 and 200 tonnes of carbon to the atmosphere. Chopping down part of a rain forest has an additional effect: when the canopy of trees is removed the earth warms and releases methane.

Methane has a powerful greenhouse effect, 20 times as much as carbon dioxide, but it is less important because there is much less of it and it stays in the atmosphere for only 10 to 12 years. It has more than doubled in concentration in the atmosphere since 1750, but there are still only some 1.7 parts per million. It is produced by many human activities, in natural gas, as a product of decaying organic matter, and – a point that newspapers have been quick to pick up on – cattle and sheep flatulence. Other greenhouse gases were already identified as pollutants for different reasons: nitrous oxides and CFCs. Hydrofluorocarbons are powerful greenhouse gases, several thousand times more potent in their greenhouse effect than CO_2 and although the quantity is small their use will increase because they are the ozone-friendly substitute for CFCs. Environmental protection often produces these trade-offs, with something that protects our environment in one area damaging it in another.

Several governments responded to the Toronto clarion call with promises that they would reduce CO_2 emissions, like people in a burst of enthusiasm making New Year resolutions that are destined to fade from the memory as the months go by. West Germany (as it then was) said it would reduce its CO_2 emissions by 25 per cent by 2005; East Germany matched it with a promise to cut emissions by 20 per cent by 2000; Sweden and Belgium said they would reach 1988 levels by 2000; The Netherlands said it would stabilize emissions by 1995 with a 2 to 3 per cent reduction by the end of the century; Canada, less ambitiously, said it would stabilize at 1990 levels by 2000 'as a first step'; Britain set itself the still more modest target of 1990 levels by 2005.

But not everyone was going to heed the global fire alarm call and rush to the pumps. The issue was already becoming politicized. This became clear when James Hansen's testimony before the Senate committee was published in the official record some months later. The Office of the Management of the Budget had altered his evidence, inserting two paragraphs stressing that his forecasts were based on estimates only and were not reliable predictions. Not surprisingly, he protested angrily and the passage was corrected.

The carbon dioxide issue is the CFC issue writ large. Like the ozone layer issue, it is more extensive than other international issues, both in space, affecting as it does the entire planet, and in time, extending over decades and centuries.

Governments could agree, with difficulty, to cut down on CFCs and then ban them. CFCs feature in only a small area of industry, and there are substitutes. Carbon dioxide is produced by all of industry, in fact, by everyone in their daily lives. (Apart from anything else, we breathe it out.) The amount of power we use, and therefore, if it is produced by traditional means, the amount of carbon we produce, is a measure of our wealth. Russia is producing much less carbon than it did a few years ago just because it is producing less of everything and has become a poorer country. Political leaders committed to a booming industrial society, promising voters more of the same only bigger and better, have every reason not to want to believe in global warming, and in the need to cut back on carbon dioxide emissions.

The old identification of Left and Right on the environment arose again. There is no logical connection between the anti-missile 'star wars' defence programme initiated by President Reagan and the theory of greenhouse warming. But one would expect that a think tank that championed the first would oppose the second, as indeed the George C Marshall Institute in Washington has done. It produced papers disputing the greenhouse effect thesis which found favour with John Sununu, the White House chief of staff who had argued against the idea that the ozone layer was being depleted.

Spurred on by Sununu, the Administration insisted that greenhouse warming was only an unproven theory. 'Until we have a firm scientific foundation, there is no justification for imposing major costs on the economy in order to slow the cost of greenhouse gas emissions', Sununu said, in a typical statement. President Bush said there should be global action but with the proviso that it must not interfere with economic growth or free markets.

Yet the United States is the most environmentally conscious nation in the world. Eleven million Americans belong to environmental organizations. No other country has such large, well-protected and well-managed national parks. You can drive for thousands of miles in the eastern states along roads lined with trees on both sides. Nowhere else will people leap so quickly to the defence of an obscure species of bird or gastropod that appears to be threatened. America's Clean Air Act is as rigorous as any in the world and is enforced strictly. The Conservation Reserve Program to conserve cropland is taken as a model.

Prime Minister Margaret Thatcher stepped forward, and came out strongly for action on climate change. This was a surprise. The most ideologically committed Conservative prime minister that Britain has had in the 20th century, a strident patriot and nationalist, dedicated to the free market economy, she turned out for a while to be also a strong and globally minded environmentalist. There has been speculation ever since about the reasons for her stand. Her scientific background undoubtedly played a part; she took a degree in chemistry at Oxford and worked as a chemist for a food company before becoming a lawyer. Some say she saw the emergence of green political parties in European politics as straws in the wind.

A major influence, certainly, was Sir Crispin Tickell, who was Britain's ambassador to the United Nations. A career diplomat, he is also an amateur naturalist and scientist. When he was seconded to Harvard University for a year, a privilege given to a few high-flying Foreign Office officials, he chose to study, not an aspect of international relations, but what was seen then as an eccentric choice, climate change in history. The resulting book, *The Influence of Climate in Human History*, became one of Harvard University Press's biggest sellers.

As a diplomat Sir Crispin played the game of nations, but he has the vision and imagination to see beyond the game. Soft-spoken, with a quietly authoritative manner, Sir Crispin comes from the heart of the British establishment and speaks its language, and he was listened to in Downing Street. He has continued to play a part in international environmental affairs. He is the only non-American on the US National Academy of Sciences panel on climate. He is also the warden of Green College, Oxford, where he directs environ-mental studies. (The name of the college has nothing to do with his subject matter: it was named after its founder.)

Mrs Thatcher staged a day-long meeting in Downing Street at which she had scientists lecturing her entire cabinet about the ozone layer and climate change. These issues were still far from the political mainstream, and some ministers who attended felt they were just indulging her in one of her idiosyncrasies. One minister fell asleep during the afternoon session and was reprimanded.

She staked out her position in a speech to the Royal Geograph-ical Society in London in September 1988 where she spoke about acid rain, damage to the ozone layer and climate change. 'It is possible, that with all these enormous changes – population, agri-cultural, use of fossil fuels – we have unwittingly begun a massive experiment with the system of this planet itself,' she said, echoing the words of the Toronto Declaration. 'We have to consider the wider implications for policy – for energy production, for fuel efficiency and for reforestation.' Showing that she was not turning her back on her aim of making Britain richer, she also said: 'The health of our economy and the health of our environment are totally dependent on one another'. The *Daily Telegraph* commented that this speech 'put climatic change at the top of the worldwide political agenda'. Environmentalists found in her an unexpected ally, and she forced the pace of negotiations on the ozone layer.

(Her efforts were widely appreciated. A conference on biodiversity was in progress at the UNEP headquarters in Nairobi on the day Thatcher was forced out of office. An outraged Mustafa Tolba, the UNEP director, summoned the British delegates to his presence to lecture them on the ingratitude of British people towards their great leaders. He said she was a champion of the environment. 'When I was ill during the Basle Convention negotiations, she sent me a personal hand-written letter', he told them. 'She said I had to get well because the world needed me. So I got well.')[5]

Later, Mrs Thatcher appeared to let her dedication to market forces overcome her views on the environment. She ceased to take a lead in the campaign for reducing carbon emissions and defended vigorously the individual's right to drive a car. Environmentalists had hoped she would take up the cause after she left office, but she has had little to say on the subject.

* * *

The US Congress asked for recommendations from the National Academy of Sciences, and it produced its report in 1991. It called for action but it was cautious. It said the forecast of climate warming was uncertain but added: 'It poses a potential threat sufficient to merit prompt responses'. It recommended low-cost measures to reduce greenhouse gas emissions, and defined low cost as less than $10 per tonne of greenhouse gas reduced. 'Options requiring great expense are not justified now', it said.

Even low cost was more than the Administration was prepared to pay at this point. It coined a new phase: it said it was willing to undertake 'no regrets' policies. Secretary of State James Baker explained what this meant: 'We are prepared to take actions which are fully justified in their own right and which have the added advantage of coping with greenhouse gases. They're the policies we will never have cause to regret.'

Scepticism about the greenhouse effect was not all politically motivated or malign. There were respectable reasons to doubt the thesis. The scientific consensus was neither universal nor confident. Several factors justified some reserve in accepting all the assertions about global warming. It is difficult to separate one development among the many that affect the climate and ascribe effects to it. There may be long-term patterns of which we are still unaware. Changes are taking place anyway in the planet as well as the weather system. Sea levels have been rising by about a tenth of an inch annually for the past hundred years; Britain is tilting slightly towards the south-east, Kent and Sussex sinking at the rate of one-sixteenth of an inch per year, the Scottish mountains rising at the same rate. Finally, it is on the face of it unlikely that a group of scientists convened to discuss what might be a problem would decide that there is no problem and no need for further research money, and return to obscurity.

The global climate system is incredibly complex, with many processes in the atmosphere and the seas interacting in changing ways. The many variables makes it ideal for computer modelling, and this is the principal tool for predicting the world's weather. Forecasters produce a range of models based on different data. The limitation to our knowledge is not in the modelling but in the reliability of the data and the uncertainty about effects of some changes.

Measurement of the temperature, past and present – let alone future – is fallible when one is talking of changes in fractions of a degree. How much does one allow for the fact that many observatories are located near cities, which are always warmer? The IPCC has tried to take this into account. Many of the measurements involve taking the temperature of sea water. Whether one uses a canvas or a wooden bucket to haul up the sea water makes a difference; water in a canvas bucket starts to evaporate immediately and may be several tenths of a degree cooler by the time it is measured. (Today thermometers are trailed in the water.)

Measurements can be distorted by external events. The temperature chart shows that the oceans were one degree warmer during the period 1940 to 1945. The only plausible explanation involves neither statistics nor the weather. During those years the world was at war, ships were blacked out at night, and samples of water were taken only in the daytime.

Scientists may have been pondering the uncertainties of the greenhouse warming theory, but industrialists in coal, oil and power made up their minds immediately. It was bad for business. If it was accepted, people would have to use less of what they were selling. They went into battle against the theory. Spokespersons for the fuel industry argued that greenhouse warming was only an unproven hypothesis, with all the fervour with which tobacco industry spokespersons had argued that there was no proof of a link between smoking and lung cancer. The big car manufacturers joined them, and they formed the Global Climate Coalition (GCC). And not only corporations. The United Mineworkers of America lent its weight, foreseeing that cutting back on carbon emissions would mean cutting back on coal-miners' jobs, and persuaded the rest of the labour movement to come on board. Industry's ideological driving force is seen in an article by Warren Brookes in the business magazine *Forbes* in December 1989. 'As Marxism is giving way to markets,' Brookes wrote, 'the political "greens" seem determined to put the world economy back into the red, using the greenhouse effect to stop unfettered, market-based economic expansion.'

Opinion polls showed a majority of Americans in favour of action to prevent climate change, but the GCC hired the same public relations firm that had campaigned effectively against a national health service, which was also favoured by most Americans. They warned the public that action on global warming would mean economic hardship. They made television commercials showing a driver worried about the soaring price of petrol and families appalled at their rising household bills because the global warming people have had their way. Lobbyists from the GCC attend every international conference on climate change, political or scientific, and lobby hard in Congress. It includes donors to political campaigns, who must be listened to. When any development occurs, the GCC's view is on the desk of every Senator and Congressman the same day.

The GCC publishes the *World Climate Review*, a publication dedicated to refuting greenhouse warming alarms. Any scientist who was sceptical about the greenhouse theory could get subsidies for his work and for publication of his views. Patrick Michaels, a scientist who disputes the idea that greenhouse warming is happening, testified before a congressional committee that he had received more than $150,000 in research grants from the fuel industry, including the German Coal Association, in 1993.

Dr Sallie Balunias, an astronomer at the Harvard–Smithsonian Center for Astrophysics, thought she saw a correlation between fluctuations in solar radiation intensity and climate change. She suggested in a paper at a scientific conference at La Jolla, California that this, and not the emission of greenhouse gases, might explain global warming. The GCC organized a public relations campaign to publicize her views, and plucked her out of academia to go on television and radio talk programmes across the country. Several scientists rejected her view in an article in the magazine *Science*, saying that variations in solar radiation are too small to have any effect on the world's climate.

The battlefront is worldwide. GLOBE (Global Legislators Organ-ised for a Balanced Environment) is an international organization of legislators campaigning for greater awareness of the climate change issue and calling for action whose first president was, the then Senator, Al Gore. The chairman until recently was Thomas Spencer, a member of the European Parliament. Spencer, a popular figure in the Strasbourg corridors, was vociferous in blaming climatic disasters on increased carbon emissions. 'They shouldn't give hurricanes women's names, they should name them after the fuel companies. They should call them Hurricane Texaco and Hurricane Shell!' he once said.

In February 1999, Spencer was coming back to England when customs officers stopped him and searched his baggage. They found pornographic literature and a video in his suitcase. He was fined, the case made headline news and he did not stand again. It is almost unheard of for members of the European Parliament to be stopped by customs. Spencer has never voiced in public any suspicions about who might have known what was in his bag and tipped off customs, but his friends have.

* * *

To get an authoritative scientific opinion, the UN Environment Programme and the World Meteorological Organization set up the IPCC, under the chairmanship of the Swedish meteorologist Bert Bolin, and instructed it to report to the UN General Assembly. It is still studying the climate and will continue to produce reports. Its reports represent the most wide-ranging and comprehensive investigations on climate. In fact, they represent the most wide-ranging scientific investigations on anything; there has never before been a group of scientists from so many countries conferring continually. The Royal Institute of International Affairs in London, an organization not given to hyperbole, said of the IPCC: 'It has evolved into what is probably the most extensive and carefully constructed intergovernmental advisory process ever established in international relations.'[6]

Its estimates on climate change, produced for the UN, are the canonical view of the subject, the ones which governments accept as the basis of policy. It produced its first assessment, a massive document in three volumes, in 1990, an interim report in 1992, in time for the Rio conference, and another at the end of 1995. It is due to go on reporting. Each volume contains a summary of the findings for policy-makers.

The IPCC was divided at the start into three working groups, the first to study the science of climate change, the second response strategies, and the third the economic and social dimension. Its process is so cumbersome that it seems remarkable that it gets any agreed results. In each working group there are up to 14 specialist groups dealing with separate issues. In Working Group 1, for instance, there are groups addressing the carbon cycle, the polar ice caps and sea levels, among other subjects. Each separate report has to be approved and commented upon by all the members, going round again and again, and then submitted for peer review. Members work with the available evidence: the IPCC gathers no evidence of its own.

To chair the first group, the Scientific Assessment Group, Bolin chose Sir John Houghton, the director of the British Meteorological Office. A veteran committee man, he has been a physicist and astronomer and is also the author of a book on the relationship of science and religion. This was a daunting task since no one knew quite what was involved. The work was unpaid but brought scientists into the area of public policy. Some rose to the occasion. A Canadian scientist on the panel, asked to serve for another two years, replied with a letter filling an A4 sheet of paper setting out what the work had cost him in stress and in time that could have been spent on his own research and with his family. He concluded: 'Of course I'll go on. It's the only worthwhile thing we do.'

The IPCC was supposed to be a completely objective study, unaffected by political considerations. Fat chance. By now the subject had become highly political, particularly the areas of Working Groups 2 and 3, which would suggest who might be hurt by climate change and what might be done about it, what the report calls 'response strategies'.

Indeed, some scientists felt that Bolin himself was hardly being the neutral, detached scientist when he told the lead authors before they wrote the summary: 'We must write this report in such a way that the policy-makers will come to the right conclusions'. As one said, 'We weren't in much doubt about what the right conclusion was'. Bolin has always made his position clear. He told the Rio conference: 'Our scenarios show that more far-reaching efforts are required than are now being contemplated in order to achieve a major reduction in the rate of carbon dioxide increase in the atmosphere'.

The principal political pressure came and still comes from the oil-producing Arab states. Their motive is commercial self-interest. Reducing carbon emissions means cutting back on oil consumption, so they disputed the thesis that putting carbon into the atmosphere is making the world warmer. The chairman saw early on that the reports not could be put to a formal vote because the oil-producing states would be a barrier to any progress at all, so they are arrived at by what was called consensus.

For a time the Saudi delegate to the Scientific Working Group was a lawyer who argued like a lawyer. Confronted with an unpalatable scientific conclusion, he objected and said to Houghton, 'I gave way on the last point. You should give way on this one'. Houghton tried to explain that a scientific conclusion is not arrived at by negotiation. Often the Saudis are simply obstructive, holding up meetings for hours with procedural arguments. The Saudis and Kuwaitis can be counted on to call for qualifiers to any conclusions, watering them down with words like 'probable' and 'possible' and 'could be'.

The Arab States had powerful allies. The US government still played down warnings about climate change, and the Soviet Union saw itself as an oil and natural gas exporter. When a sentence in the draft report began, 'We calculate with confidence', they wanted to drop the words 'with confidence'.

A key figure helping the Gulf oil states is Donald Pearlman, a former under-secretary in the Department of the Interior during the Reagan Administration, now a Washington lawyer with a lobbying firm, working closely with the GCC. A heavy-set, jowly, chain-smoker, Pearlman is known as 'Deputy Dawg' to some of the participants for his relentless pursuit of any argument and hectoring manner. He once startled a British scientist by warning him that there would be 'blood on the carpet' if a certain paragraph appeared in the report. Pearlman attends every meeting, sometimes with some assistants. Kuwaiti emendations have appeared on papers in his handwriting.

When scientists and government ministers met to thrash out the final report at Sundsvall in Sweden in August 1990, a new view was heard, from the representatives of one of the smallest countries. Peter Timeon is the foreign minister of Kiribati, a group of tiny Pacific islands with its capital on Tarawa atoll, scene of one of the most terrible battles of World War Two. He broke into a day of wrangling over wording to tell them in sombre tones what was at stake for Pacific islanders: 'In the low-lying nations, the threat of global warming and sea level rise is frightening . . . There is no place among my country's thirty-three atolls that rises more than two metres above sea level. Long before the sea level rises that far, my country and others like it will have been condemned to annihilation.' His words were received in silence and when he had finished speaking many delegates broke into applause, the only time this happened during the conference.

Although the IPCC did not set out its report in this way, there were two questions that needed answering: is the world getting warmer, and is human activity responsible? The IPCC answered yes to both, and forecast that the rise in temperature will continue whatever we do, because of the gases that we have already put into the atmosphere.

The 1995 report broadly confirmed the findings of the earlier one. It said with greater certainty that we are making the climate warmer; 'more signals are appearing among the noise', as one member put it. The central conclusion in the summary is: 'The balance of evidence suggests that there is a discernible human influence on climate'. The members of Working Group 1 worked over this sentence for hours at their final meeting in Madrid. Was 'discernible' the right word? Would 'indicates' be too weak? Would 'shows' be too strong? Some wanted to say there was a 'substantial' or 'significant' influence. The Saudis and Kuwaitis did not like 'discernible'. They wanted to insert a reference to 'preliminary evidence which is subject to large uncertainty' but this was rejected.

The report laid out the long-term effects of the build-up of greenhouse gases: concentrations will rise and the weather will become warmer because of the gases we have emitted already. The 1990 report said that to stabilize concentrations of carbon in the atmosphere at today's levels would require an immediate reduction of our emissions of more than 60 per cent. The 1995 report did not give any such figure, not because it had re-calculated but because talk of a reduction on this scale in the near future is unrealistic. The second report reduced slightly the level of warming expected. This was because the authors took into account the effect of aerosols, the sulphate particles emitted as industrial smoke which block out some of the sun's rays. (Ironically, clean air legislation increases global warming by removing these.) It also reduced the effect of CFCs.

The reports contain projections, not predictions. That is, they forecast what will happen *if* the emission of greenhouse gases is at such-and-such a level. The main projections are based on business as usual: what will happen if the emission of greenhouse gases continue at their present rate. As it turns out, they have not continued at this rate. The yearly increase has levelled out and emissions have even fallen slightly, although not enough to halt the warming process or avert the consequences.

The consequences as foreseen by the IPCC include flooding, the spread of diseases to new areas, an increase in storms, desertification, water shortages, the loss of biodiversity and damage to crops, with the probability of improved crops in some places before the damage begins. Many cities now in a semi-tropical climate belt – in southern Europe and in the American south, for instance – will experience new diseases, a rise in heat-related deaths, and a strain on electric power supplies needed for air conditioning and refrigeration. In most of America, unlike Europe, warmer weather means that more power is used because of widespread air conditioning.

The effect on food crops is varying. Some crops will grow better with an increase in carbon in the atmosphere. In some greenhouses, growing tomatoes in Britain, for instance, additional carbon dioxide is pumped in. But any improvement may be followed by adverse effects on the crops, such as water shortage and an increase in pests. In some places the land will dry up, but some land too cold for farming now will become arable. The arable area will move 125 to

200 miles northwards for each degree of warming. Some farmers may have to change their crops if they are to survive. There are a few near-certainties: vegetable crops will improve in Europe, maize crops will fall in southern Asia, and millet crops will fall in Africa, both crops essential to the present diet of the local population. But with most crops in most places, the IPCC says they could increase or decrease; it does not know which.

The poor will suffer most from the change, as they usually do. The 1995 report says: 'Many of the world's poorest people – particularly those living in subtropical and tropical areas and dependent on isolated agricultural systems in arid regions – are most at risk of increased hunger. Many of these at-risk populations are found in sub-Saharan Africa; south, east and Southeast Asia; and tropical areas of Latin America.'

The reports were supplemented by an interim report, in 1997, breaking down the effects by regions of the world. Africa, it turns out, is the most vulnerable continent. Political and social factors as much as the extent of climate change are major indicators of damage, partly because of the limitations they place on the ability to adapt. In the case of Africa these are listed as 'deterioration in the terms of trade, inappropriate policies, high population growth rates and lack of significant investment'. It forecasts a serious spread of infectious diseases and says international action will be necessary to tackle Africa's health problems.

Europe will face flooding in the northern part of the continent and drought in the south. By 2100, 95 per cent of Alpine glacier mass may have disappeared. China will face flooding and water shortages, but the prospects for its agriculture are very uncertain: there is likely to be a fall in its main crops, rice, wheat and maize, but it is possible that other crops will do better with the climate change. In Latin America, water shortages will reduce livestock.

Any climatic change will be a delayed effect of the increase in greenhouse gases. It will result from things we are doing now. If we reduce the emissions of greenhouse gases, whatever effects are produced will go on and will only taper off after a period of years.

Working Group 3, on the social and economic impacts of climate change and of mitigation measures, concluded, as others have done, that emissions can be reduced in most countries at little or no cost: 'no regrets' measures. It went on: 'The risk of aggregate net damage due to climate change, considerations or risk aversion, and application of the precautionary principle provides rationale for action beyond no regrets'. It recognizes the wide area of uncertainty and says: 'The challenge is not to find the best policy today for the next 100 years, but to select a prudent strategy and adjust it over time in the light of new information'.

A later report by forecasters at Britain's Hadley Centre in November 1999 confirms the IPCC's findings and adds new warnings. It says the temperature could rise even more over continental land masses and most of the Amazon rain forest could disappear. Emissions must be reduced.

None the less, a start has been made. The message put out by the IPCC and amplified by many others is being heard.

CHAPTER 3

WHO DOES
WHAT?

Great waves looked over others coming in,
And thought of doing something to the shore
That water never did to land before

Robert Frost[1]

SOME 13,000 YEARS ago, northern Europe
suddenly became much colder. The average temperature fell by
5 degrees centigrade over a period of less than 50 years, a single
lifetime. The last Ice Age had ended, the glaciers that had once
covered much of Europe and North America had been retreating
for thousands of years, and the ground was green and covered with
forest. Now something approaching Ice Age conditions were
coming back.

One can only imagine the effect on our Cro-Magnon ancestors
who lived there. They were hunter-gatherers. In the Middle East,
Homo sapiens had begun to cultivate crops and to live in settled
communities, but not in Europe. The effect of the extreme cold
spell must have been terrible. The frost and snow would have come
earlier each year, and become fiercer each winter. Vegetation would

have been killed off and animals would have migrated or starved. Men and women would have roamed through the forests that covered most of the continent looking for the fruits that once sustained them and finding only a poor shrivelled version, hunting animals that were becoming fewer, and getting hungrier and weaker as the winters grew longer, with more of them dying each year.

If such a sudden change occurred today it would be the greatest natural disaster in human history. It would cause almost unimaginable hardship in the countryside and in the cities, and it would also have worldwide climatic effects. Yet this could happen.

It was known for some time that this abrupt climate change occurred in about 11,000 BC, but only recently has an explanation been found: the ocean currents. In normal times, warm water flows up from the Gulf of Mexico across the Atlantic. The colder, saltier water flowing down from around Greenland is denser and so it sinks, allowing the warm current to flow northwards above it. This is the Gulf Stream. In the 1950s oceanographers tracing the radioactive tritium released in nuclear bomb tests in the Pacific found that this is only a part of a transglobal circular ocean current.

The Gulf Stream carries an enormous amount of heat and this warms the atmosphere. It is because of the Gulf Stream that Europe is warmer than other parts of the world at the same latitude, that Dublin, Manchester and Hamburg have a more comfortable climate than Goose Bay, Labrador, although they are all at latitude 53.30 degrees North.

Professor Wallace Broecker, a geochemist at the Lamont-Dohert Institute for Atmospheric Research in San Diego, has worked out from geological evidence what happened in 11,000 BC, and his explanation is now widely accepted. Paradoxically, Northern Europe became colder because the world was becoming warmer. When the Ice Age glaciers retreated, they left a large inland sea in Canada.

It was held there by an ice dam in what is now Lake Superior. As the temperature rose, the ice dam melted and the cold water from the inland sea poured into the North Atlantic, overwhelming the Gulf Stream. The North Atlantic, instead of bringing warmer weather to Europe, brought colder weather.

Some 1300 years later, there was an equally sudden reverse in the ocean currents. Europe became warmer within a few years, with decreased rainfall. It is less clear why this happened, but once again this would have played havoc with the crops on which people depended for their existence.

Scientists at the Potsdam Institute for Climate Impacts Research have detected signs of the same process that sank the Gulf Stream, an increased flow of cold fresh water into the North Atlantic. The cold water has come, not from an inland sea left over from the Ice Age, as it did in 11,000 BC, but from melting ice in Greenland and the North Polar region. They reported their alarming findings at one of the major conferences on climate change, in Buenos Aires in November 1988. Stefan Rahmstorf said, 'There is a threshold in the North Atlantic ocean circulation beyond which the circulation may collapse abruptly. We may reach that threshold early in the Twenty-Second century. But it could be much sooner.'[2]

One can expect an additional source of fresh water if warming continues, from increased rainfall and snow in northern latitudes. Cold fresh water will not sink like the cold salty water but will remain on the surface, disrupting the global circulation pattern.

Uncertainties abound. The British Meteorological Office considered the question. It said that its latest models show that at most, the Gulf Stream might slow down, but the loss of heat to Europe will be more than offset by atmospheric warming.[3] So we can relax on that score. But then the next paragraph said: 'Some other climate models show a more drastic reduction in ocean circulation, and the reason for this range of responses is not understood'. So perhaps we can't.

It turns out worryingly that over the past few hundred thousand years, such flip-flops are a regular feature of the climate, and may require only a small push. Taking a long-term perspective, the world's weather over the past 10,000 years, during which civilization developed, has been unusually stable. Occasional sudden changes are the rule, not the exception. If we are changing the climate, the change is likely at some point to become abrupt. As Wallace Broecker says: 'Earth's climate does not respond to forcing in a smooth and gradual way. Rather, it responds in steep jumps which involve large-scale reorganization of the Earth's system. This is much more difficult to deal with.'[4]

The world's climate system is non-linear. This means that cause and effect cannot be represented by a straight line, the same amount of cause always producing the same amount of effect. A change can produce a small effect but, carried on, this can turn into a larger effect, or else dwindle away. The system is, in the technical sense, chaotic. A chaotic system is one that is so complex and so sensitive to inputs that there is no consistent and predictable connection between cause and effect. Indeed the classic example used to illustrate chaos theory is a meteorological one: a butterfly flapping its wings in Peru starts a chain of events that ultimately causes a hurricane in China.

Scientists working on the IPCC are now paying more attention to the likelihood of abrupt changes in weather patterns. In March 1998, the IPCC organized a workshop at Noordwijkerhout in The Netherlands on rapid non-linear climate change. Two French scientists, Jean Jouzel and Jean-Claude Dupressy, set the tone with their paper: 'The paleoclimatic record has provided multiple examples of how the climate system is capable of unprecedented abrupt change . . . It is only during the eighties that the possibility of such changes, occurring at the timescale of human life or less, was fully recognised, thanks to the ice core drilled at Dye 3 in Southern Greenland.'[5]

Another paper said a change to warmer weather is usually more rapid than a change to cooler weather: 'The paleoclimatic record suggests that the time-scales associated with cooling are generally longer than those with warming. A typical . . . cycle consists of a cooling phrase of several hundred to a thousand years, then a cold phase of a few hundred to a thousand years, followed by an abrupt warming of a few decades or less.'[6]

Of the several kinds of sudden events, a major shift in the Gulf Stream would be the most catastrophic, and this was one that was considered. Another is a sudden surge in warming of the atmosphere, at a rate much too fast for people to adjust.

At the end of the conference, one of the senior scientists taking part said that it is now accepted that a sudden and drastic change in the weather due either to a shifting of ocean currents or to some other cause is possible. Pressed for a quantitative assessment of the likelihood, he guessed that if carbon emissions continue at their present rate, there is a 1 per cent chance in the next ten years, 5 per cent in the next 50 years, 10 per cent in the next 100 years and 25 per cent in the next 150 years.

James Hansen, who caused a stir with his testimony before a Senate committee in 1988, has now changed, if not his mind, at any rate his tone, emphasizing the element of uncertainty. 'The forcings that drive long-term climate change are not known with an accuracy sufficient to define future climate changes', he wrote in a recent article.[7] 'Climate modeling and forecasting needs to be rethought . . . Uncertainties in climate forcings have supplanted global climate sensitivity as the predominant issue.'

Electricity Daily, the trade paper of the American electricity industry, reported this gleefully under the headline 'Hansen Recants On Warming'. But Hansen denies that he has recanted, and explained what he meant. 'The evidence is clearer now that the world is getting warmer. But we don't have enough evidence to know how much. The concentration of CO_2 is flattening out. Forests and soils have taken up more. The concentrations of methane is slowing down for reasons that we don't understand.'[8]

He is certainly not suggesting that there is no danger. 'We should take action. We're conducting an experiment with the atmosphere, and we should slow it down. If you go ahead full blast, you increase the chances of a surprise event', he said.

Meteorologists rarely use the term 'global warming'. It is too simple, too crude a term to encompass the phenomenon. It does not begin to describe the many different kind of changes that can come: storms, more rain here, less there, much warmer here, possibly cooler there. They speak instead of climate change.

Media reports of the IPCC findings usually consist of forecasts without qualifications and uncertainties. But because of the nature of the weather system, its complexity and its sensitivity to inputs, scientists have little confidence in precise predictions. Indeed, the most alarming thing about the IPCC reports is not the confident assertions, of which there are very few, but the great uncertainties about what is going to happen. The forecast usually given for temperature rise is what will take place if our greenhouse gas emissions continue to increase at the 1995 rate, what the IPCC calls the 'business-as-usual' scenario, meaning a steady increase in carbon dioxide emissions of about 1.5 per cent per year. The business-as-usual scenario would mean a warming of 0.2 degrees centigrade for each decade, resulting in a rise of about 2.5 degrees centigrade over 1990 levels by the end of the 21st century, and this is the figure usually quoted.

But this figure of 2.5 degrees centigrade is little more than a guess, a mean figure taken in the middle of a range of uncertainty. What the report actually says is that the temperature will rise between 1 and 4.5 degrees centigrade. It also says that the rise is not likely to be steady but will proceed in spurts. Furthermore, it says the rise will not be uniform but will vary in different areas.

The biggest unknown is cloud cover, which could produce either positive or negative feedback. The IPCC says: 'The range in estimated climate sensitivity is largely dictated by this uncertainty'. Warmer air means more water vapour and hence more clouds. But what kind of clouds? High altitude clouds trap heat and so enhance the greenhouse effect: positive feedback. Low altitude clouds shield the earth from the sun's rays and so have a cooling effect: negative feedback. The current best estimate is that 3 per cent more high altitude clouds would raise the temperature by 0.3 degrees centigrade, and 3 per cent more low clouds would cool it by 1 degree centigrade. We don't know what kind of clouds will be created.

In fact water vapour, which constitutes 1 per cent of the atmosphere, is a much more potent greenhouse gas than carbon dioxide, whether clustered in clouds or dispersed in the air. Climate scientists do not know how to factor in the water vapour effect in a changed atmosphere.

As the world becomes warmer, sea levels will rise, although this will not happen quickly because the seas respond slowly to temperature change. This may well be the most important long-term consequence of climate change and the most disastrous for many people. It is particularly important because, since the oceans store more heat than the atmosphere, the delayed effect of sea level rise is even greater than that of change in the air temperature. If the build-up of greenhouse gases in the atmosphere were to stop in 2030, sea level rise would continue for the next 70 years. It is a problem we will leave for our grandchildren.

How much will the sea level rise? Pick a number. The IPCC report says its best estimate is that with continuing emissions sea levels will rise by 50 centimetres – that's just under 2 feet – over the next century. This is the forecast usually quoted. But this also is only a figure in the middle of an extraordinarily wide range of uncertainty. The report says the rise could be as low as 15 centimetres or as high as 95 centimetres.

The biggest single cause during the next few years will be the thermal expansion of water. Water, like everything else, expands as it becomes warmer. The melting of mountain glaciers and their running down into the sea will be only a small factor in the immediate future, but as the years go on this will also raise sea levels. After that comes the melting of a part of Greenland's ice cap and the Antarctic ice. Arctic ice melting will affect the weather but not the sea level since it is floating ice. In Antarctica, warmer weather may mean less ice melting, and this is the kind of paradox that occurs in the global climate system. Warmer weather will mean more water vapour, which in cold weather will come down as snow. The snow will provide a protective cover for the ice that will prevent it melting.

The albedo effect can produce feedback. Albedo is the reflection of the sun's radiation. Ice reflects the most sunlight of all. As ice melts, less heat is reflected and more is absorbed. If carbon content were doubled, the reduced albedo would increase warming by 20 per cent. This would melt more ice which would mean less reflection which will mean more heat absorbed. And so on. This would be a runaway positive feedback, reinforcing and speeding up the warming process.

The permafrost which covers millions of square miles may also be a big source of positive feedback. Permafrost is the permanently frozen ground which extends over much of Siberia, northern Canada and Alaska. Underneath it are huge amounts of bacteria. If permafrost melts, these bacteria will be exposed to the air and will emit methane into the atmosphere. There is also methane locked up since the last Ice Age in gas hydrates, a mixture of water and organic waste formed at low temperatures and high pressure. The methane will contribute to the warming process, which will cause more of the permafrost to melt, which will expose more bacteria and more methane. And so on once again.

Billions of tonnes of methane hydrates are under the Arctic seas. If the sea becomes warmer and this starts to melt, the coal industry could take second place as an emitter of greenhouse gases.

Living things have always interacted with the atmosphere and still do. The IPCC tells us: 'Changes in vegetation can potentially further modify climate locally and regionally by altering the exchange of water and energy between the land surface and the atmosphere'. However, the kind of effect that will ensue turns out to be an area that we do not understand: 'Coupled atmosphere-ocean models used for climate change studies do not yet include such interactions'.

A change in plant life brought about by warming can feed back into the carbon cycle, and it seems that it might do so. Or, on the other hand, it might not. 'Sustained rapid climate change could shift the competitive balance among species and even lead to forest dieback, altering the terrestrial uptake and release of carbon. The magnitude is uncertain, but could be between 0 and 200 GtC (that's 200 billion tonnes of carbon) over the next one or two centuries.'

The albedo effect comes into play here also. Some kinds of ground reflect more sunlight than others: dry earth reflects more of the sun's rays than vegetation, and water more than land. Hence, as the IPCC says, 'Forests spreading into tundra in a warmer world would absorb a greater proportion of solar energy and increase the warming'.

The report forecasts climate change in different areas: greater warming than the global average in the central United States with drying-out in summer (drought, bad for crops) but more rain in winter, more rain and more damp in southern Asia (good for crops), summer-time drought in southern Europe, and more. But then it all but destroys these forecasts with a single sentence: 'Confidence in these regional estimates is low.'

The 1990 report says: 'Although many of these feedback processes are poorly understood, it seems likely that, overall, they will act to increase rather than decrease greenhouse gas concentrations in a warmer world . . . For this reason, climate change is likely to be greater than the estimates we have given.' It is surely unusual for a scientific report to arrive at an estimate, and then say in a later paragraph that the real figure is likely to be higher. This has the sound of a conclusion reached by a committee, stretched out of shape to try to satisfy a lot of different people.

All these factors will interact, multiplying the uncertainties. As the IPCC concludes: 'Unexpected large and rapid climate system changes as have occurred in the past are, by their nature, difficult to predict . . . Future climate changes may involve surprises'. In matters concerning our environment, surprises are bad news.

In adding to the greenhouse gases in the atmosphere, we are heading into unknown territory. We are tinkering with a powerful mechanism that we don't understand. Reading the IPCC reports with their multiplying uncertainties, the Toronto declaration about a dangerous experiment with the planet comes to mind.

* * *

Shortly after the first IPCC report was published, Mrs Thatcher opened the Hadley Centre of the Meteorological Office at Bracknell, Berkshire, 40 miles from London, to serve as the British end of the IPCC. With her penchant for extended metaphor, she said at the opening: 'We have a full repairing lease on the Earth. With the work of the IPCC, we can now say we have the surveyor's report, and it shows that there are faults and that the repair work needs to start without delay.'

There was no doubt what 'repair work' the faults identified by the IPCC required. We have to cut down on the emission of greenhouse gases, principally CO_2. Creating CO_2 by combustion is at the heart of most electric power supply, industry and transport. Who is going to do the cutting down, and by how much? That is the big question of global environmental politics today.

Even if there were an abundance of goodwill behind the project, it would be difficult to devise a scheme to share out equitably the responsibility for cutting back on carbon emissions. How much should the United States cut back compared with European countries? Americans are profligate with their fuel; taxes on fuel are so low that the price is a third of what it is in most European countries. America emits twice as much carbon as countries such as Britain and Germany per unit of industrial output. But America is a much bigger country, things have to travel over longer distances, and it covers several climate belts.

Why should France cut back, when it already emits much less carbon than other industrialized countries because it gets 75 per cent of its electricity from nuclear power, which burns no fossil fuel and produces no carbon? Should the poorer countries of the European Union, Greece and Portugal, be asked to cut back as much as the richer members? Surely the requirements of a huge, thinly populated country like Australia, where goods, electricity and people have to travel vast distances, must be different from the more compact, crowded countries of Europe? Japan is already the most fuel-efficient country in the world. Should its already lean industry be asked to reduce while others have only to trim their fat?

And what about the developing world? The industrialized countries have become rich by burning fossil fuel. They have created the problem. Are the countries trying to develop their industry, many of them struggling against hunger and deprivation, to be told that they must slow down their development while people in the richer countries, the big carbon emitters, enjoy their heated swimming pools and air-conditioned cars?

There is a glaring disparity between the greenhouse gases emitted by the industrialized nations and the others. The industrialized countries contain only 20 per cent of the world's population, but their power plants, factories and cars pour out 80 per cent of the carbon that the world is putting into the atmosphere. The United States alone emits 22 per cent. Britain (population 57 million) emits 3 per cent, hardly more than India (population 870 million). The disparity becomes clearer if one looks at emissions per capita. The average American produces 6 tonnes of CO_2 to maintain his way of life, the average British person 3 tonnes, a Chinese 0.7 tonnes and an Indian 0.25 tonnes.

This means that the West's actions have been the principal cause of the climate change damage so far, including the increase in storms, from which developing countries have suffered most. The charity Christian Aid spelled out the significance of this in terms of equity and justice, in a report in September 1999. The report says the West owes the world's poorest countries hundreds of billions of dollars in environmental damage. 'We constantly think of the world's poorest countries as being in debt to us,' a Christian Aid spokesman said presenting the report, 'and force them to adopt draconian economic austerity measures as a result. But these debts are dwarfed by the huge and rising carbon debt owed by the rich countries to the global community, and for which, yet again, the poorest are paying.'

But the developing countries are catching up fast. Most countries' carbon emissions have increased but those of the developing countries have increased faster as they industrialize and modernize. America's carbon output increased by 10 per cent between 1990 and 1998, but Brazil's increased by 25 per cent, China's by 30 per cent and India's by 37 per cent. China and India in particular have huge coal reserves; in the 1990s China exceeded the United States as the world's leading coal producer, and 75 per cent of its commercial power comes from coal. If large industrializing countries such as China, India, Pakistan, Indonesia and Brazil continue to develop at the same rate and in the same way, and use coal as their principal source of power, the increase in carbon emissions will overwhelm any reductions the developed countries manage to make half-way through the 21st century.

How to organize a worldwide cutback is the issue before us. It was first forced on to the international agenda at the Conference on Environment and Development, dubbed the 'Earth Summit' by the media, in Rio de Janeiro in June 1992, the 20th anniversary of the Stockholm conference on the environment. Brazil was eager to host the conference partly to counter its image as an environmental bad guy for its destruction of much of the Amazon rain forest. Inevitably, the climate change issue took centre stage. This is not what the developing countries wanted. They wanted development, meaning aid of one kind or another, at the top of the agenda. The title of the conference linked the two. The biggest single item on the agenda was Agenda 21, a 600-page action plan for helping the developing world achieve sustainable development and greater equity. The product of much serious thought, it would have meant an increase in Western aid among other things, and has not received much governmental attention.

The United Nations (UN) General Assembly charged member countries with producing a Framework Convention on Climate Change, the FCCC, in time for the Rio conference. With new scientific evidence coming all the time, the idea was to have a flexible agreement, a framework into which figures and other details could be inserted and changed as circumstances required.

A series of preliminary meetings were held, and here the line-up became clear. Most Europeans wanted to press ahead with targets and a timetable. But the Americans argued against commitments to reduce carbon dioxide or even setting targets. Prime Minister John Major sounded a note of disappointment. 'The world looks to the American Government for leadership on this issue as on others', he said. As pressure mounted, the Bush Administration made placatory gestures: it announced reforestation programmes, and pointed out that America's clean air legislation removed greenhouse gases from the atmosphere.

A bloc of industrialized nations formed that stood out against commitments and, when they became inevitable, tried to minimize them. It came to be known as JUSCANZ, an acronym formed out of the names of its members: Japan, the United States, Canada, Australia and New Zealand. All are wealthy nations, and all except Japan are large with thinly populated areas and profligate in their use of fuel.

The Soviet Union said little, and it was not only because it saw itself as a potential oil exporter. A leading Soviet meteorologist had persuaded the government that the Soviet Union, and particularly Russia, stood to gain from a warmer climate, that any loss would be more than offset by the opening up of vast areas of frozen waste in Siberia to agriculture. This view has largely been superseded by events but it still bursts out occasionally. During an unseasonably, warm December the deputy director of the Institute for Global Climate and Ecology, Igor Nazarov, told a reporter: 'In

fifty years time the volume of greenhouse gases will double. Permafrost, which occupies 58 per cent of our territory, will start to
melt. In the central part of Russia, good conditions will appear for
agriculture, and there will be drought in the United States. Then it
will be their turn to sweat for food!'[9]

In fact given the climatic and other uncertainties, it would be
unwise for any country to count on profiting from a warmer world,
particularly as damage to agriculture elsewhere would make it a
more unstable world internationally. As it happens the situation
has changed and Russia now stands to make money out of an
international agreement to reduce carbon emissions.

Most of the developing countries either remained sceptical about
climate change during the run-up to Rio, or refused to contemplate
taking any steps to remedy it. A typical view was set out by the
then Indian foreign minister, Chandras Dasgupta, in a BBC television programme: 'The process of development in the South
will require increasing use of energy, and that means increasing
levels of per capita emissions of carbon dioxide. . . There can be
no restrictions placed on developing countries, whose levels of
carbon dioxide are far lower than developed countries. The responsibility for limiting and stabilizing emissions of greenhouse gases,
and in particular carbon dioxide, must rest with the developed
countries.'

However, one group of developing countries called for urgent
and strong action. This was the Association of Small Island States,
AOSIS. The founding members were island nations in the Pacific
and Indian Oceans that are particularly vulnerable to sea level rise
and to an increase in storms. Many Pacific atolls are also threatened
by the shrinking of coral reefs as the sea becomes warmer; the
coral reefs act as a sea barrier. As the IPCC said, in curious phrase-
ology, 'With some island nations the effects could be very severe,
including non-existence in the worst cases'.

As if to illustrate the point, the representative of the Maldive Islands, Ismail Shafeen, told a climate change meeting: 'Three years ago, for the first time in our history, written or traditional, the islands were flooded, inundated by huge swells. This took place across 600 miles of islands. It destroyed houses and agriculture . . . We never believed that the sea could do this to us. It brought home to us that the world is changing.'

Thirty-five members now make up AOSIS; they are not all small and picturesque Pacific atolls: they include Singapore, Cyprus and Malta. They called for the Toronto target of 20 per cent reduction of the 1988 level of carbon emissions by 2005 until this became totally unrealistic, and they are still urging strong action.

The Rio de Janeiro conference was the biggest summit meeting ever held, with 118 heads of government and state attending and some 30,000 others, including 10,000 journalists. A notable feature was the presence of non-governmental organizations, which meant mostly environmentalist pressure groups. Maurice Strong, the Canadian chair of the conference and of the Stockholm conference 20 years earlier, set out to ensure that they had a place, and some have played a role in the ongoing discussions. The conference was about many things beside climate change, and the discussions covered the whole area of environment and development, but the two urgent environmental issues were climate change and the loss of species.

The Framework Convention on Climate Change represented the best they could do given the need to get the United States on board. It remains the framework within which all negotiations on curbing climate change are going ahead. The convention acknowledged the need to cut greenhouse gases in its statement of aims: 'Stabilization of greenhouse gas concentrations in the atmosphere, at a level that would prevent dangerous anthropogenic interference with the climate system. Such a level should be achieved within a time-frame sufficient to allow ecosystems to adapt naturally to climate change, to ensure that food production is not threatened, and to enable economic development to proceed in a sustainable manner.'

This accepted that there will be climate change, but aimed to keep it down to a rate that would allow people to adapt. If, over decades, the weather in southern England becomes too warm and the ground too dry to grow strawberries, fruit farmers there may grow grapes or even oranges. But they would need a lot of time to adjust and make the change. Cities would have to adjust their services.

Each signatory to the convention promised to 'take measures on the mitigation of climate change by limiting the anthropogenic emissions of greenhouse gases and protecting and enhancing its greenhouse sinks and reservoirs'. 'Sinks' and 'reservoirs' are areas of plant life such as forests, and the oceans that soak up and retain carbon. Signatories also agreed to produce accounts of their emissions and plans to reduce them.

The authors of the convention avoided specific commitments to reduce. They tiptoed around even the modest target which had been suggested, of reducing to 1990 levels of greenhouse gases by the year 2000, with some fancy verbal footwork. One paragraph said – and this only applied to the developed countries – that the aim should be to 'return by the end of the decade to earlier levels of anthropogenic emissions'. The next paragraph referred to 'the aim of returning individually or jointly to their 1990 levels'. The phrases 'end of the decade' and '1990 levels' were not in the same paragraph. Most of the developed countries did not return to earlier levels of emissions by the end of the decade; their emissions went on rising.

The convention also endorsed what has come to be known as the precautionary principle: 'Where there are threats of serious or irreversible damage, lack of full scientific certainty shall not be used as a reason for postponing cost-effective measures to prevent environmental degradation'.

Despite its very limited commitments, the convention has had long-term effects. It required parties to submit accounts of their emissions of greenhouse gases, and also of the absorption of carbon by carbon sinks. This sometimes involves more developed countries using their technology to help others to monitor their emissions. To ensure that it is an ongoing process, it called for periodic reviews of the adequacy of these commitments 'in the light of the best available scientific information'. The parties were to meet annually to work out ways of furthering the aims of the convention. It is at these meetings that the current schemes are being thrashed out, and the machinery of this new kind of international cooperation is being developed.

Like the ozone layer agreement, it established two classes of nation, the Annex 1 group, the developed countries, and the Annex 2 group, the others. The Annex 1 group are to take the lead in any reductions in emissions. However, this division was rooted in history rather than present-day reality. Some of the Annex 2 countries are now wealthier than some in Annex 1. Singapore and Korea were included among the developing countries, Russia and Ukraine among the developed. This was to have significant consequences.

The convention follows the precedent of the agreement on the ozone layer in a number of other ways. Its structure is the same: a protocol into which specific obligations with numbers and dates are to be slotted in, as governments can agree to them and in the light of changing scientific knowledge. It calls for a regular review of commitments. It uses independent scientific assessment. It has provisions for international assistance and technology transfer.

The Interim Fund set up to channel international assistance on the ozone layer now became the Global Environment Facility

(GEF), with a mission to deal with climate change as well. The GEF funds projects in developing countries in four areas where the planetary environment is threatened: depletion of the ozone layer; loss of biodiversity; pollution of the seas; and the build-up of greenhouse gases. It is administered jointly by the World Bank, the UN Environment Programme, and the UN Development Agency, and run from offices in one of the World Bank buildings in Washington. It has $2.75 billion to spend during the current four-year period. The United States is behind with its payments to the GEF, as it is to other UN bodies, because some key members of the Senate Foreign Relations Committee deem it unpatriotic to subscribe to international organizations.

The GEF divides its projects into two types. Type 1 are those in which the cost-benefit analysis comes out favourably for the country concerned, so that it would pay the country to do it regardless of any environmental impact. An example of this is the supply of 1.7 million energy-efficient light bulbs in two provinces of Mexico, which has brought down the cost of lighting, and incidentally reduces the amount of electricity used and hence carbon emissions. A Type 2 project is one in which the cost-benefit analysis is favourable to the planet but not to the individual country, so that a subsidy is required. Examples of this type are the setting-up of a 32-megawatt power plant in Bahia Province, Brazil, using eucalyptus tree chips as fuel, and the supply of solar-powered electricity in Rajasthan, India, both creating power without burning fossil fuel. It is hoped that these will one day become economically viable, with improvements in efficiency and economies of scale in manufacturing.

Unlike some other international aid organizations, the GEF goes in for small-scale projects, most of which can serve as pilots at which their technical and financial viability can be assessed. For instance, it distributed energy-efficient cooking stoves in Benin, West Africa, and off-grid solar cell electricity systems in Zimbabwe. These means that local people have to chop down fewer trees for firewood.

The Rio conference, for all its shortcomings and disappointments, established the big picture on climate change. It was broadly accepted that we are changing the climate and this can cause damage to us and to future generations. We know what to do. It was also accepted that in the initial phase at least, it is up to the industrialized countries to clean up the mess they have created. The GEF was a step in this direction. The Framework Convention remains just that: the framework within which all international agreements on reducing emissions will be negotiated.

Having established what needs to be done, governments are now working on the nitty-gritty of who is going to do it.

CHAPTER 4

SOME NITTY-GRITTY

International arrangements may change qualitatively because those who participate in them change their minds about interests and aims, usually because of changes in information available to elites or new knowledge otherwise attained – Donald Puchala and Raymond F Hopkins[1]

The bargaining process created by such a structure will be inherently messy, and will produce political compromises that do not reflect the optimal, most cost-effective approaches to stabilising greenhouse gases – William A Nitze[2]

IN THIS UNUSUAL situation, there are several possible kinds of international action. For those with a penchant for taxonomy, we can categorize them.

One is **unilateral**. A country may decide unilaterally that it will reduce its carbon emissions as a contribution to the general good. As we have seen, unilateral action was the first American response to the discovery of the damage to the ozone layer, a domestic ban on aerosols containing CFCs, and other countries followed suit. This was also one response to the Toronto Declaration on global warming. Canada, Germany, The Netherlands and some other countries announced that they would cut their emissions by fixed percentages for the good of the planet. The EU promised unilaterally to reduce its emissions and has set dates and timetables.

This can be important as a trail-blazer, particularly if some countries either fail to ratify the protocol or fail to fulfil the commitments to which they have agreed. It shows what can be done. As Richard Benedick, the chief American negotiator on the ozone layer treaties, has written: 'When influential governments make such a commitment they legitimize change, and therefore undercut the argument that change is impossible.'[3]

Another kind of action is what one can call **multi-unilateral**, or **reciprocal**. It means doing something in the expectation that another country will respond, or else in response to what another country does, but without a formal commitment on either side. There are precedents for this kind of tacit agreement. During the first nine months of World War Two, Germany and the Western allies held back from bombing each other's cities. All sides during the war refrained from using poison gas although most had the means to do so. More recently, when the US Senate refused to ratify the comprehensive nuclear test ban treaty, the Clinton Administration announced that it would keep to its terms anyway and hoped others would do the same, and they have done so. The British government recently waived the debts of the world's poorest countries, following the failure of the Organization for Economic Cooperation and Development (OECD) countries to agree on more than limited debt relief measures, and asked others to follow suit.

One advantage of this kind of tacit arrangement over a formal one in a democracy, and this certainly applied to Cold War arms control measures, is that it does not have leap the hurdle of ratification by Parliament or Senate. The US Senate has not ratified the 1998 Kyoto Protocol on climate change. A disadvantage in a democracy, if the issue concerns something that industry rather than government does such as emitting carbon, is that a head of government, if he or she makes a promise to reduce emissions, may find it difficult to ensure the necessary measures are taken.

There may also be moral pressure on a government to reciprocate. Moral pressure is not often cited as a factor in international affairs but it should not be discounted, particularly if it is exercised through the medium of public opinion. Sir Crispin Tickell spent most of his career in the British diplomatic service and can be expected to be realistic and hard-headed in his view of international behaviour. He wrote in his book on climate change: 'No government flourishes under a prolonged international disapproval. Few even enjoy casting a veto in the Security Council. In the last resort, policing an agreement on climate as on other aspects of the environment would depend on the translation of a consensus of opinion into means of mobilising, persuading and if necessary shaming governments into co-operation and compliance.'[4]

The next stage is **contractual**, a binding treaty committing governments to work towards greenhouse gas reductions. This is the aim. Voluntary reductions and tacit agreements may work for a time. But in the long run, the world can no more rely on voluntary reductions in greenhouse gas emissions than a government can dispense with taxes and rely on voluntary contributions from its citizens. The contract that is on the table now is the Kyoto Protocol, the international agreement negotiated in Kyoto in December 1998 on reducing greenhouse gas emissions. One weakness of the protocol is that there are no penalties for non-compliance.

A sub-class of contractual is **contractual plus sanctions**, and this would include such penalties. In the longer term, it is hoped that the treaty will be broader in scope, for it is only part of an ongoing process. The sanctions against signatories who do not fulfil their obligations would presumably be trade sanctions, but they must be serious enough to be a deterrent against non-fulfilment and also applied vigorously enough so that any country, however powerful, could be subjected to them.

Such a treaty would have more than the normal sanctions against those who break it. It would also include sanctions against non-joiners, the free-riders. Any agreement must come up against the problem of the free-rider, the equivalent of the non-tax payer in a society, who enjoys the benefits of others' efforts while refusing to contribute himself. All the more so if in this case, the non-participating country becomes a haven for industries that want to pour carbon dioxide into the atmosphere in a way they are prevented from doing in their own countries.

A treaty with sanctions against non-participants shades over into the next possibility, **eco-hegemony**. This would be a response to a desperate situation. It might apply in a situation of impending disaster. Major powers agree on a scheme for reducing emissions. They are unable to reach agreement with others on what is to be done. With the world facing ecological catastrophe, they take military action to prevent others from frustrating their efforts, perhaps with United Nations approval.

International conferences on climate change seem to be high on drama. Preliminary meetings to thrash out negotiating points usually leave many issues unresolved. There are late-night sessions or all-night sessions and frayed feelings. There are almost always cliff-hangers, with the possibility of a breakdown of negotiations. Here is an account by the British diplomat Tony Brenton of a meeting in Sundsvall, Sweden: 'Having started in a very civilised fashion with songs about the future from children's choirs and an address from the prime minister of Sweden, the meeting . . . finished at four o'clock in the morning one day late with most of the delegates having abandoned their chairs to stand on the podium and shout at each other.'[5]

Another characteristic of these conferences is the conspicuous presence of two groups of non-governmental organizations, or NGOs. On one side there are the environmentalists, many of them young enthusiasts dressed in jeans and trainers and staying at b&bs. Some of the more energetic among these sometimes stage demonstrations, climbing a building to unfurl a banner, or releasing balloons carrying their message. Others, older and more conservative in their tactics, buttonhole whatever delegations will listen to them. They play an important role. One NGO, the Climate Action Network, linking several national and international organizations, produces a daily news-sheet at the conferences, *Eco*. This provides a useful, if admittedly subjective, report of events, including interviews with delegates. The Climate Action Network has on occasion been a channel for unofficial negotiations between parties.

On the other side there is the GCC and its industrial allies, and Donald Pearlman and his acolytes, the 'carbon club', professional lobbyists in business suits, staying at business hotels, inviting delegates to lunch or drinks. Both these groups have the attention of delegates, with their noises off and sometimes noises on, for representatives are allowed to sit in on the sessions and sometimes to speak.

The Framework Convention called for an annual Conference of the Parties after it was ratified by the requisite number of countries, and the first of these, known as COP 1, was held in Berlin in March and April 1995. It was supposed to come up with something more specific to put into the framework, but at 12 preparatory meetings the civil servants had not been allowed to agree to any specific measures. The chairperson in Berlin, German environment minister Angela Markel, proved to be stern and invigorating. 'If we are serious about long-term change, we will not be able to avoid radical alterations in our life style', she warned the delegates at the opening.

In America George Bush had been replaced in the White House by Bill Clinton. Clinton's vice-president, Al Gore, was an earnest advocate of action on the environment, and had written a book on this theme, *Earth in the Balance*.[6] Gore had criticized the Bush Administration's attitude to climate change as 'an abdication of leadership'. None the less, the Republicans controlled Congress, the Western world had just been through a mild economic recession, and the undersecretary of state for global affairs, Timothy Wirth, came to Berlin to resist demands for new commitments. So far as the US was concerned, there were to be no specific targets or timetables; indeed these words were to be avoided. The JUSCANZ alliance – Japan, United States, Canada, Australia and New Zealand – held firm.

The EU wanted commitments. John Gummer, Mrs Thatcher's environment minister, now believed passionately in the need to curb global warming. He told the meeting angrily: 'We are no longer talking about the effect on our grandchildren but on our children – and that means American children too!'

Several developing countries now agreed that carbon emissions must be reduced but said the West should do the reducing. The Indian environment minister, Kamal Nath, described carbon emissions in Western countries as 'luxury emissions', and said those in developing countries are 'survival emissions'.

The developing countries are grouped in what is called, for historical reasons, G77, after the fashion of the G8 nations, the eight wealthiest countries in the world that have regular economic summits. The original 77 countries have now become more than

100, and since China stands apart they are usually called G77-plus-China. They rarely share a common viewpoint, since they include countries as disparate in their situations as the Association of Small Island States, calling for strong action, and the Organization of Petroleum Exporting Countries (OPEC) countries calling for inaction. The smaller developing countries often produce problems because their delegates to the conference usually deal with many environmental issues and cannot be up-to-date on the specific details under discussion. All too often they will vote against something simply because their home governments do not know enough about it.

The International Chamber of Commerce was represented at Berlin, and they issued a statement opposing any action. The fuel industry lobbyists and Donald Pearlman and his minions were rushing in and out of the negotiating room to put the pressure on delegations and stiffen resistance to calls for carbon reductions. They were so intrusive that the chairman eventually barred NGOs from the negotiating floor.

Five days into the conference, the *New York Times* correspondent reported: 'It seems unlikely to produce substantial progress'. But at an all-night session, a combination of Ms Markel's firmness, the Europeans' pressure, the OPEC opposition's exhaustion and the American delegation's bold decision to go further than Congress wanted, all produced a document that allowed the process to go ahead. The document came to be called the Berlin Mandate.

It said the measures agreed upon so far were inadequate, and that the parties were to set objectives of limiting and reducing emissions within specified time frames beyond the year 2000. It also set up a secretariat for the Framework Convention in Bonn (where there would be plenty of office space going spare since the German capital was moving to Berlin), two subsidiary bodies to implement it and a budget.

If they had not set targets and timetables, they had at least agreed implicitly that they would set them. They were inching towards action. Timothy Wirth said this was the best outcome imaginable in the circumstances, with which the environmentalists would reluctantly agree, and he added, in a witty historical reference, 'Now we can say, "*Ich bin ein reducer*".'[7]

The opposition kept up the pressure. President Clinton received a letter signed by 119 heads of most of America's biggest industrial corporations, including Amoco, Chevron, Chrysler, Exxon, Ford, General Motors and Texaco. 'The US should not agree to any of the three proposed protocols presently on the negotiating table', the letter said. 'Your leadership on this issue is critical to assuring a continuing strong US economy'. Pressure from this source could not be ignored.

Governments are not monolithic, and the arguments between governments were and still are paralleled by the arguments between government departments. In London and Washington and in the European Commission and elsewhere, government departments defend their constituencies. Ministries of commerce, trade and industry argue over environmental action with ministries of the environment and foreign affairs. Views are heard, interests taken into account and positions worked out.

After the Berlin meeting the Clinton–Gore Administration turned its attention to the climate issue. It brought a number of prominent environmentalists into government. Jessica Tuchman Matthews, Rafe Pomerance of the World Resources Institute, David Gardiner of the Sierra Club and several other prominent figures in environmental organizations were given appointments in the Administration, although some of these were soon to leave. Spurred on by Gore, the Administration reversed its stand.

It announced its new policy at the next Conference of the Parties, COP 2, in Geneva in July 1996. Wirth called for a legally binding agreement to cut emissions after the year 2000. He denounced 'the naysayers and special interests bent on belittling, attacking and obfuscating climate change science'. He must have felt liberated in saying this, for these were the very forces that had held him back from supporting strong measures earlier.

By now the IPCC's second assessment had appeared, with its 'clearly discernible signs of greenhouse warming' paragraph, and its warning of 'dangerous interference with the climate system'. OPEC still disputed its findings. Saudi Arabia's Mohammed Saban insisted that the science was still uncertain and said the next IPCC assessment might warn of the dangers of global cooling, which was received with incredulity.

With American support, the emissions reduction process was now rolling forward. In Geneva, COP 2 ended with a declaration that went beyond the Berlin Mandate. It instructed delegates to draw up a legally binding protocol setting targets at the next meeting, in the Japanese city of Kyoto in December 1997. This was to be the crucial meeting.

When Tony Blair spoke at a special session of the UN General Assembly on the fifth anniversary of the Rio summit in June of that year, a few weeks after becoming British prime minister, he issued a warning: 'We in Europe have put our cards on the table. It is time for the special pleading to stop and for others to follow suit. If we fail at Kyoto we fail our children because the consequences will be felt in their lifetime.'

America seemed to have deserted JUSCANZ, and with Japan changing its policy, Australia and New Zealand were isolated in still opposing any action on climate change. Clinton rubbed the point home when he visited Australia shortly afterwards. Standing in a park in Queensland, he said, 'If present trends continue, there is a real risk that some time in the next century, parts of this very park could disappear, submerged by a rising ocean. That is why today, from this remarkable place, I call upon the community of nations to agree to legally binding commitments to fight climate change. We must stand together against the threat of global warming. A greenhouse may be a good place to raise plants; it is no place to nurture our children.'

* * *

During all these discussions and negotiations, concepts have been developed, and mechanisms also, which will be the basis for international action.

One of these is joint implementation. Under joint implementation, two countries will act together to reduce the carbon dioxide level. This means one country, usually the United States or a Western European country, spending money in another to reduce the carbon content in the atmosphere, either by making a carbon-emitting facility such as a power plant more efficient, or by planting trees which absorb the carbon. The donor country would then expect to get credit for the amount of carbon reduced in any international agreement on who has reduced by how much. A rich country can usually get more carbon out of the atmosphere by spending a given amount of money in a poor country than at home.

A lot of this has gone on already. The United States established a Joint Implementation Initiative in October 1993 and has so far undertaken 25 separate projects costing $450 million, in Latin America and Russia. Thirteen of these involved renewable energy and 12 tree-planting or preservation. Some companies engage in the initiative to get credit for their green credentials and also, perhaps, at some future date, credit against reducing emissions when this is required. Applied Energy Services planted 52 million trees in Guatemala at the same time as it opened a coal-fired power plant in Connecticut, calculating that those trees will soak up all the carbon the power plant puts into the atmosphere. Costa Rica has embraced the idea enthusiastically, welcoming projects and establishing an office for joint implementation.

Western European countries have carried out their joint implementation schemes in eastern Europe. The Scandinavian countries are carrying out projects in the Baltic states, with which they have many ties stemming from their geographical proximity. They have enabled power plants to switch from coal to natural gas and have made coal-fired plants more efficient. The Dutch state electricity company charges a small levy to pay for its programme of planting trees abroad, to absorb some of the carbon it is emitting.

Joint implementation sets efficiency against equity. It may be efficient to reduce emissions in the places where it is easiest or cheapest to do so, or even to plant trees to absorb the carbon. But it goes against people's intuitive idea of equity, for it allows the wealthier countries to avoid taking action of their own. An American environmentalist, Irving Mintzer, compared it to the practice in the American Civil War by which a man could avoid being drafted into the army by paying for someone to take his place. Asian countries have often been resistant to the idea – India has refused to accept any joint implementation projects.

The objection on equity grounds was voiced angrily by an African after hearing an account of a tree-planting scheme. 'Why should African governments let their land be used as a toilet for absorbing emissions from Americans' second cars?' he demanded.[8]

An Indonesian environmentalist, Agur Sari, pointed out that even much of the carbon emissions in developing world countries was for the benefit of Western consumers. 'The mistake', he said, 'is in identifying greenhouse emissions *in* a country rather than *by* a country. Emissions produced by a Southern country in manufacturing goods to be consumed by people in the North are counted as a Southern country's emissions.'

A practical objection raised by some developing countries is that joint implementation would use up the easiest carbon reduction options, so that when developing countries come to take measures they will find it more expensive. Some environmentalists have pointed out that there is no guarantee that the trees planted will be maintained, or that they will not be cut down at some future date. If they die, then the carbon they have absorbed will be released back into the atmosphere. None the less, joint implementation in one form or another is going to play a bigger part in any international moves to reduce emissions.

Another idea is tradeable emissions. This is the international development of an ingenious scheme that has been in place in the US since 1992 as part of the Clean Air Act and has proved very successful. It was introduced as a measure to reduce emissions of sulphur dioxide, a major industrial pollutant. The principal mechanism is not regulation, which American business does not like, but market forces, which it does. The Department of the Environment sets a limit each year on the total amount of sulphur dioxide that can be emitted. This is then apportioned out among the industrial plants that are the emitters. Each is given its yearly quota, and a measuring device is put on its chimneys, to be taken off and checked on New Year's Day to ensure that it has not exceeded its quota. Currently, the fine for exceeding the sulphur dioxide limit is set at $2500 for each ton above the quota, a high enough figure to discourage carelessness.

However – and this is the novel part – if an industrial plant reduces its output by more than is required, exceeding its quota of reductions, it can sell the difference. That is, if it is allowed to emit 10,000 tonnes and it has cut its emissions to 9000, it can sell the permit to emit 1000 tonnes. So another industrial plant can decide whether it is cheaper to, for instance, put scrubbers on its boilers to remove 1000 tonnes of sulphur dioxide, which apart from the initial cost means paying a price in energy efficiency, or to buy another company's quota for 1000 tonnes. The price is set by supply and demand.

This system means that the emissions of pollutants will be cut in the most economical way; the company that can reduce its emissions more cheaply than another will do so, and the other will find that it is cheaper to buy the reducing company's extra quota. Administrative costs are small because the market is self-regulating. And the authorities can decide each year what is the total amount of pollutant that is allowable.

Trading began in 1992, and in the following year auctions of sulphur dioxide quotas began, conducted by the Chicago Board of Trade. The price slid from $130 to $150 a tonne of sulphur dioxide in 1992 to below $70 in 1996, reflecting the lower-than-expected cost of reducing emissions, although it has climbed again since then. Reduction of sulphur in the air has exceeded the target. When the Montreal Protocol on CFCs was passed, the Environmental Protection Agency (EPA) set up a trading system for these also, and this reduction also exceeded the target. Now plans are afoot to adapt this system to carbon reduction, to make international trading in carbon emissions a part of the regime to reduce climate change.

Tradeable emission quotas is practised only in America, yet the first plan to adapt it to global carbon emissions was drawn up by an Englishman, Michael Grubb, in a paper published by the Royal Institute of International Affairs in 1990.[9] Under this scheme, quotas would be allotted to a country solely on the basis of its adult population. Thus, a country like India, with a large population and a relatively small industrial capacity, would have quotas to spare to sell to the West, which would have every incentive to reduce its emissions so as not to have to buy more. The system would tend towards equilibrium, the final point at which each country's emissions would be proportionate to its population. The scheme was ingenious, logical and fair. But these qualities are not the most relevant ones in drawing up rules for international behaviour. It never had a chance of being accepted because it would have meant a massive flow of funds from the West to the developing world in payment for emission quotas.[10]

* * *

American opponents of action on climate change continued to argue that cutting down on carbon dioxide would cost American industry dear in money and in jobs lost. Now they pointed out that the Climate Change Convention was saying the industrial countries would have to give a lead. Playing on the longstanding American fears about losing jobs to cheap labour countries, they said this would mean America and its allies doing all the reducing while developing world countries reaped the benefit. Partly in response to this pressure, the Senate passed a resolution, the Byrd–Hagel Resolution, by 95 votes to none, saying that it would not ratify any agreement that did not include action by developing countries. This was to overshadow the negotiations at Kyoto, and it has overshadowed discussions ever since.

In the run-up to the Kyoto meeting, the opposition tone became more shrill. The GCC warned readers in another advertisement: 'We could pay 50 cents more for every gallon of gasoline and 25 to 50 per cent more for natural gas.' This was to be expected. Another full-page advertisement on the eve of the Kyoto meeting was not anticipated. It appeared in the *Wall Street Journal*, which had consistently expressed scepticism about climate change, and was signed by 60 leaders of major corporations. It was headed: 'Get Serious About Climate Change', and it urged the US Administration to take a lead in promoting measures to reduce greenhouse gas emissions. Among the signatories were Ted Turner and the heads of Bechtel and Evron. This signalled a change in the attitude of industry.

Insurance industries were among the first to come out on the side of action. Climate change is bad for the insurance business. Insurance losses from weather-related disasters have soared. In 1981, measured in 1997 dollars, they amounted to $600 million; in 1998 they were $15 billion. (The peak year was 1992, when losses were $25.1 billion.) Much of this increase is due to changes in lifestyles, people becoming wealthier and building more expensive properties in areas susceptible to storms and flooding, such as Florida and the Caribbean islands. But much is due also to the increase in storms. European insurance industries issued calls for action. The American insurance industry would not join in.

The 1995 IPCC report carried a warning, not just for the insurance industry but for the whole financial sector. The report on the impact of climate change carried a chapter, unlike the 1990 report, on the impact on financial services. Its conclusion was grim: 'Changes in climate variability and the risk of extreme events may be difficult to detect or predict, thus making it difficult for insurance companies to adjust their premiums appropriately. If such difficulty leads to insolvency, companies may not be able to honour insurance contracts, which would economically weaken other sectors, such as banking. There is a need for increased recognition by the financial sector that climate change is an issue which could affect its future at the national and international level.' American insurance companies refused to take this as seriously as their European counterparts.

Some major fuel companies have decided to go with the flow, and have begun deserting the GCC line. British Petroleum, Shell and Texaco are all starting to invest in non-fossil fuel power, such as solar power and wind power. Although at the moment this is only a very small part of their investment, this seems to be less a cosmetic device – although they all make great play with their green credentials – than an attempt to ensure that they are not left behind if the pattern of power generation changes. These companies are hedging their bets. The Edison Electric Institute (EEI), representing 600 electrical utilities in America, broke ranks with the GCC with a go-with-the-flow statement: 'We sell electricity and we don't care where it comes from', said EEI president Charles Linderman. 'The power lines don't know whether it comes from coal, wind or solar cells. We are with the future.'

As is normal at international climate meetings, delegates went to Kyoto with some points still not settled and with many doubtful about whether they would reach an agreement, which was required of them by the Berlin Mandate. The Europeans wanted a timetable for reductions. The Americans agreed but very cautiously, and they did not want to start soon. British environment minister John Prescott was influential in hammering out a compromise. As at previous meetings, some delegates from Britain's EU partners muttered privately that the British were 'in the Americans' pocket', as one put it, although Prescott is clearly too abrasive and too volatile to be contained in anyone's pocket. The Europeans accepted reluctantly a delayed starting-date, and the others accepted the aggregation of EU members' emissions so that they could be considered together.

The American plan was for commitments among the industrial-ized countries – Annex 1 countries, in the terminology of the Climate Convention – to reduce emissions by the period 2008 to

2012, with the possibility of deferring reductions. They also wanted flexibility in the way countries met these commitments, allowing for trade in emissions and joint implementation; flexible mechanisms, or 'flex-mex' was the key phrase. The Americans also wanted plans for voluntary reductions by the developing countries: Annex 2 countries. Most developing countries were against plans even for voluntary reductions, seeing this as a step in the direction of commitments. The Europeans wanted more ambitious targets, the Japanese less.

The GCC had 63 lobbyists at the conference including representatives of the petroleum, coal-mining and automobile industries, fighting to prevent an agreement. They had the support of some members of Congress who were in Kyoto. Seeking allies where they could find them, GCC lobbyists worked on the Indian and Chinese delegations, urging them to stand firm against Western proposals. The *New York Times* correspondent reported: 'The private sector lobbying, more intense, prolonged and costly than usual in the realm of diplomacy, has reached a fevered pitch this week in Kyoto.'

The conference followed the pattern of previous ones, with furious arguments in the corridors, hectic late-night sessions, and constant fears that attempts to reach an agreement would fail. President Clinton telephoned the leaders of Argentina, Brazil and the Philippines to urge them to compromise on their positions. Thirty delegates were admitted to hospital suffering from exhaustion and dehydration.

The last sticking point was emissions trading. Developing countries wanted limits on all flexible mechanisms, to ensure that the industrialized countries reduced their emissions. The Europeans did also, but not so severe a limit. So far as America was concerned, flex-mex was the basis of any reduction commitments. The Administration felt it could not sell Congress on the idea of forcing American industry to make deep cuts in its carbon emissions, and that it could only get the reductions by getting credit for reductions in other countries.

The climax was a hectic, all-night session at which American delegates at one point were standing on their chairs trying to get the chairman's attention, other delegates were asleep with heads on their desks and their headphones beside them, while others were sitting in the aisles because there were not enough seats. Chairman Estrada thrashed out with the principal parties a compromise resolution with some deliberately imprecise wording, which put off decisions on thorny details. He ignored objections and put it to a vote a few minutes after ten in the morning. Some delegates reeled away in an exhausted daze, confessing that they were not sure just what they had voted for.

The protocol deals with the six principal greenhouse gases: carbon dioxide; methane; nitrous oxide, which is produced by fossil fuel use and in pesticides; HFCs, which are a substitute for CFCs and are therefore increasing in use; petrofluorocarbons, a substitute for some CFCs and halons; and sulphur hexafluoride. They are all important. The last three together constitute 1.15 per cent of all greenhouse gases, but each is a much more potent greenhouse gas than carbon dioxide. Sulphur hexafluoride, for instance, is 24,000 times as potent as CO_2 and has a lifetime of 3200 years.

The baseline year is still 1990. The US is to reduce its emissions to 7 per cent below the 1990 level between the years 2008 and 2012. The EU is to reduce by 8 per cent, and Japan by 6 per cent on the ground that Japanese industry is already more carbon-efficient than any other. This means reversing the present trend. Taking the IPCC's business-as-usual model, the US would increase its emissions by more than 28 per cent by 2010 and the EU by 26 per cent.

The EU gained the right to have its members' emissions calculated together, in what has come to be called the 'bubble'. Members of the EU made their own commitments within this bubble to achieve the overall reduction of 8 per cent. The poorer countries, Greece, Ireland, Portugal and Spain, will be allowed to increase their emissions as they develop their industries – by up to 27 per cent in the case of Portugal. Others are required to make reductions. In some cases these are large but can be accommodated because, as was said before, emissions levels have fallen below 1990 levels anyway: in the case of Germany because of the closing down of much of East German industry with unification, and in the case of Britain because of the shift from coal to gas. France, which has low carbon emissions because it relies on nuclear power for most of its electricity, is not required to make any reductions at all.

Australia is not required to make any reductions and in fact is allowed to increase its emissions. Its delegation argued that its 1990 emissions were unusually high because of large land clearances. Everyone is to draw up plans for further reductions beyond 2012. There are no provisions for sanctions in the case of non-compliance.

Annex 1 parties (they are called Annex B parties in the protocol, but are in fact the same) can trade emissions in order to fulfil their commitments, but trading must be 'supplemental to domestic action', a phrase that was to give rise to arguments. The rules on trading are to be decided by the Conference of the Parties in the future.

The G77 countries would not accept joint implementation as it is practised as part of the Annex 1 countries' reductions. So joint implementation is allowed only between Annex 1 countries. However, something akin to joint implementation between developed and developing countries was created in the treaty. This is called the Clean Development Mechanism. It came about through some ingenious re-packaging of a Brazilian plan which was rejected immediately by the industrialized countries, but was welcomed by everyone when it was presented in a different form.

At one of the preliminary meetings to work out the Kyoto agreement, Brazil proposed that fines be levelled on any Annex 1 countries that did not meet their commitments, and that the money be put into a Clean Development Fund. This money would be used to help developing countries limit their emissions and adapt to climate change. The G77 countries backed the proposal, but the Annex 1 countries refused to accept a system of fines for non-compliance.

However, it was difficult to dismiss entirely the idea of the fund. Under the Climate Convention, the developed countries are required to help countries that are particularly vulnerable to climate change to adapt. The GEF was contributing to reducing emissions, but nothing so far had been done to help countries to meet the cost of climate change.

Then someone had an idea. The Brazilian scheme for fines for non-compliance meant that a developed country would pay money into a fund if it failed to reduce its emissions to a certain level. Suppose a country was allowed to pay money into the fund *instead* of reducing below a certain level. It would not be called a fine for non-compliance but the effect would be the same. This was acceptable to everyone, although details have still to be worked out. To Annex 1 countries, it was joint implementation under another name, but it had to have another name because joint implementation was unacceptable to the others. The fund is to be administered by an international council, and will help countries adopt more environmentally friendly policies and also adapt to climate change when it comes.

'Sinks' will have to be calculated in these schemes. These are living systems that absorb carbon dioxide: plants and forests. The oceans are the biggest sinks, but no one can claim credit for them and the amount of carbon they absorb is not known.

There is a catch that ensures that much of the Western countries' reductions could be purely nominal. Russia and the Ukraine are classed as Annex 1 countries. Their economies have collapsed. They are producing much less than they did in 1990 and therefore emitting much less carbon. They have carbon reductions to spare, reductions that have come to them through economic and societal failure rather than by intention. The United States and other Western countries could buy them and get credit for reducing their emissions, instead of actually reducing its own emissions by that amount. Carbon reductions would be below 1990 levels. But most of the reductions would have been made already.

As was to be expected, the modest reductions called for in the treaty met with a violent reaction from its opponents. The executive director of the GCC, William O'Keefe, called it 'a terrible deal', and warned that when it comes before the Senate for ratification, 'business, labour and agriculture will campaign hard and will defeat the treaty'.

These days, when New York City is sprayed as a defence against tropical disease and every year sees new record temperatures, the opposition to action have given up trying to persuade us that climate change is not happening, and have shifted over to saying that we will enjoy it. The Cato Institute, a conservative think-tank in Washington DC which has supported the anti-climate change thesis, recently published a book by Patrick Michaels, a scientist who wrote a paper that was rejected by the IPCC forecasting booming agriculture and prosperity in a warmer world. In a recent article in the magazine *American Outlook* Denis T Avery said global warming 'might actually be a boon for the environment'. They point to the benefits of warmer weather and the signs of increased prosperity during the medieval warm period.

Certainly climate change will bring some benefits, to agriculture in some areas, for instance. A few people may be able to look forward to sitting at an outdoor café and enjoying the warm zephyrs at a time of the year when they are now sheltering inside. But the rise in temperature already matches or exceeds that in the Middle Ages, and forecasts say it will make the world warmer than it has been at any time in the last 100,000 years.

Given the evident harm that is coming, the difficulty of adjusting to rapid change, the many uncertainties, and the possibility of catastrophic surprises, it would be to say the least unwise to welcome climate warming. Anyway, the world will certainly continue to get warmer for a while whatever we do, so we will see.

The Kyoto Protocol, over which the mountains laboured mightily, will go only a little way to reduce global warming. It falls a long way short of what the IPCC says is necessary to reduce climate change. Even if it comes into force, it will only slow the build-up of carbon in the atmosphere, not halt it or reverse it. It will be only a first step in reducing carbon emissions, and a small first step. The next steps, after the first decade of the 21st century, will have to include measures by the developing countries to reduce their emissions, and more serious measures by the industrialized countries as well.

However, whether in the end it is accepted or not, when future historians look back on the first phase of the efforts of nations to manage the planetary environment together, the Kyoto Protocol will be a milestone.

5

WHAT PRICE
THE WORLD?

*'What?' said Oprubile to the interpreter. 'You have voted a war
with that rapidity and indifference?'*
*'Oh, it is an unimportant war which will hardly cost eight million
dollars.'*
'And men . . .'
'The men are included in the eight million dollars' – Anatole France[1]

*Economists state their GNP growth projections to the nearest tenth
of a percentage point to show that they have a sense of humour* –
Edgar R Fiedler[2]

CARBON IN THE atmosphere now has a
price. It is worked out in terms of the damage its presence in the
air causes by warming the climate and also the cost of reducing
the amount being put into the air, for the received wisdom is that
reducing carbon emissions will mean either switching to more
expensive sources of energy or using less. The market will set the
price if or when tradeable quotas begin, and the best guess is that
this will be between $10 and $20 a tonne. The US Department of

Energy has set aside $18 million to finance schemes for sequestering carbon. The cost of sequestering it can be up to $15 per tonne.

Questions of how much we should do and how much effort we should put into preventing damage to the environment, or repairing damage to the environment, are longer-range and more amorphous than most than come into the realm of policy. But at some stage these must be given shape and defined. At one level they are economic questions requiring a quantitative answer. How much can mean, literally, how much? How much is it worth? How much should we pay? To some, even to ask these questions about the environment is objectionable. It is like putting a price on springtime or valuing love in pounds and pence. We sense that some things are priceless.

Thus, a *New York Times*/CBS poll in 1991 found that 70 per cent of Americans thought that protecting the American environment was so important that 'standards cannot be too high, and continuing environmental improvements must be made regardless of cost'. That sounds as if the environment really is priceless. But hold on. Do these 70 per cent of Americans mean it, or is this just the sort of unthinking response that shows how shallow opinion poll results can be? Do people really think standards *cannot* be too high, and improvements must be made *regardless of cost*, sacrificing any amount of wealth, comfort and health care to make even a minor improvement in the environment? Will they really write out a blank cheque on their own bank accounts? If not, if the cheque is not to be blank, then it must have a figure.

Economists have developed tools for costing things that do not normally come with a price tag. One is willingness to pay. How much would you pay for this? Another is willingness to accept compensation. How much would you accept to give this up? Both these criteria can be applied to the environment. People can be asked:'What are you willing to pay to preserve this?' Or, alternatively, 'What would you accept as compensation for this environmental damage? How much would you want in exchange for dirtier air, for the removal of a local park, for the extinction of a species?'

This criterion is subjective. Different people will provide different answers. Some people value a splendid view more than others. The parents of an asthmatic child will be willing to pay a lot more for cleaner air than their neighbours. An opinion poll on the preservation of species found that Americans would each pay $1 to preserve the whooping crane, $6 to preserve the bluenose dolphin, and $11 for the bald eagle. Why so much for the bald eagle? Why is it worth 11 times as much as a whooping crane, a more elegant and picturesque bird? Most Americans will never see a bald eagle in the flesh. But it is a symbol of America, found on a dollar bill and on many national emblems. The same kind of attachment heightened German concern about acid rain damage to the forests that feature so large in German folklore and myth.

We have barely begun to learn how to price things as an aspect of the global environment. In Brazil, trees are cut down to clear land for resettling. The Brazilian government says a settler earns on average $300 a year from a hectare of the new land. This is what those trees are worth to the settler. (Actually, they are worth less because there are other inputs, principally labour.) A hectare is 2.47 acres. An acre of trees cut down means that between 100 and 200 tonnes of carbon remains in the atmosphere that would other-wise be absorbed. The price of carbon in the atmosphere is estimated to be between $10 and $20 a tonne. Taking a median in every case – that is, assuming that the trees release 150 tonnes per acre and the price is $15 a tonne – then the value of the land in carbon emitted comes out at $5558. This is what those trees are worth to the world. In the most simple economic terms, we should find a mechanism by which we can pay for those trees to remain in place. This is what joint implementation is.

Studies of attitudes show that peoples will always want more in compensation before they will accept environmental damage than they will be willing to pay for environmental improvement. They put a higher price on the clean air they have than on the clean air they could get, and so want more in compensation for dirtier air than they will pay for cleaner air. This is in line with other studies, on war and aggression, which show that people are more ready to fight to defend what they have than to fight in order to gain more. People are loss-averse.

Economists have calculated how much damage global warming might cause and what it is worth spending to avoid this. Some economists are using these calculations to draw policy conclusions.

William Nordhaus, one of the first in the field, calculated that only 13 per cent of the American economy is affected by climate change. The damage caused by climate change plus the cost of adapting to it would be less than the cost of reducing CO_2 emissions, he calculated. For instance, rising sea levels will only be a problem in the long term. Over 75 years, the cost of building sea walls to protect vulnerable areas will be only 0.1 per cent of private investment over that time. Therefore, he favoured only no-regrets measures. He considered the possibility of a threshold beyond which damage will increase and concluded that we should still delay taking action: 'The high productivity of capital . . . implies that investment to slow climate change should be postponed in favour of investment in conventional capital until the fateful threshold is relatively close.'[3] (More recently, he has come out in favour of a carbon tax and modest measures.)

One thing to observe about this calculation is that it is selfish. It gives no weight to the harm that carbon emitted in the United

States inflicts on other countries while Americans protect their vulnerable areas from the consequences.

Economists dealing with environmental issues have developed tools for extending cost-benefit analysis into the future. The principal tool is the application of the discount rate. The discount rate is the obverse of the interest rate. Someone may decide that a 7 per cent interest rate, compounded annually, in a ten-year bond, is a good return on their money. They have decided that it is worth paying £100 now to have £200 ten years from now. (Seven per cent interest compounded annually will approximately double the amount in ten years.) If you look for the discount rate you ask: what is it worth paying now to in order have something worth £200 ten years from now? If something in the environment, whether it be climate, landscapes, species or whatever, is worth £200, what should we pay to ensure that it is not lost but is there for our descendants a century on? The higher the discount rate, the more value something loses with the passage of time.

One way of choosing a discount rate is to take the market return on investment. This ranges between 3 and 6 per cent for long-term, risk-free public investments. Some economists argue that it would be better for future generations, as well as our own, to invest resources to increase wealth now rather than in improving or maintaining the environment if this would cost more. The economist A Wildavsky says: 'Our duty [to future generations] lies in . . . leaving behind a larger level of general fluid resources to be redirected as they, not we, see fit.'[4] This assumes – and this has always been a safe assumption in the past – that the wealthier we are as a society, the better it will be for our children. We all benefit from the wealth of past generations.

One can also take into account the expected growth in society's wealth. For the last century, the world's wealth has approximately doubled every 30 years. On this basis, a future generation will be wealthier and more able to meet the cost of climate change. But the future may be very different. The exponential growth in population, production, human activity and environmental constraints building up now implies a historic discontinuity, so that it is risky to extrapolate from past decades. Present global trends will not continue in a straight line. The worst effects of global warming may arrive just at the time when a future generation is struggling with over-population, shortage of water and exploding urban misery, and will have fewer resources to cope with it than we have, not more.

Another way of setting a discount rate is taking what economists call 'the social rate of time preference'. This is a combination of the rate of two things, 'pure time preference', which can also be called simply impatience, a preference for having something now rather than waiting for it; and, once again, the expectation that incomes will be higher in the future. Using this method the discount is variable because the criteria are arbitrary. In economists' calculations, it varies between 0.05 per cent and 3 per cent.

Discounting raises the question of inter-generational equity, our obligation to future generations. The capital and the return go to different people. If we put money away for the future, we will reap the benefit ourselves, and we can decide how much we save and what rate of interest we will accept. But in this case we are investing, or failing to invest, to prevent damage for a future generation. This is why some people say that no discount rate is justified ethically. If we create a discount price, and therefore pay less for something than it will be worth in the future, we are depriving future generations. The economist John Broome suggests this: 'A universal point of view must be impartial about time . . . In overall good, judged from a universal point of view, good at one time cannot be judged differently from good at another.'[5]

The discount rate chosen makes a big difference over a long time-scale. If a 1 per cent discount rate is chosen, at the lower end of the impatience scale, then an aspect of the environment that is worth £1000 100 years from now will be valued at £370 today, that is, it is worth spending £370 to preserve it. If the discount rate is 5 per cent, which would be a reasonable market rate, then it is valued at only £7.60 today, and it is worth spending very little to save it. This points to another drawback in future discounting: it is not much use if we are thinking of the world we will leave to our more distant descendants. If you discount over the really long term, say, more than 150 years, then anything reduces in value so much that it is almost worthless, and on strictly economic grounds we should not pay anything other than a trivial amount to preserve it. Yet some of the most damaging effects of climate change will persist for more than a century.

It is difficult to reduce many different kinds of damage, to homes, to industry, in disruption of life and even injury, to a common monetary scale of value, but it is possible. However, when these calculations are made on a worldwide basis it becomes very questionable.

Samuel Fankhauser, one of the principal economists working on this issue, estimated specifically the damage from storms and flooding likely to come with a doubling of carbon dioxide. He came up with the figures of $61 billion in the US, $63 billion in the EU, but only $16 billion in China.[6] At first sight this seems odd. Why should the damage to China be less? China is more vulnerable to flood damage than either America or Europe and less able to provide protection for those exposed, and it has a much larger population. The answer becomes clear when these figures are translated into percentages of gross national product (GNP). This damage would amount to 1.3 per cent of America's GNP, 1.4 per cent of the EU's, but 4.7 per cent of China's. The damage to

China is much greater in terms of China's economy; the Chinese lose more but in Fankhauser's calculus, it is worth less.

Frances Cairncross, who wrote about the economics of the environment when she was environment correspondent of *The Economist*, draws conclusions from this kind of assessment. She assesses the likely damage to Western industrial societies and then goes on: 'If such figures apply worldwide, the damage caused by global warming over the next fifty years might be quite modest. However, in some poor countries, the impact of damage might indeed be greater – if the gloomiest predictions of sea level change turned out to be true, for instance, Bangladesh would be swamped and the Maldives would vanish from the map. But because of the harsh fact that property prices are so much lower in the poor world than the rich, the worldwide economic costs of climate change may not be substantially different.'[7]

This is indeed a harsh way of looking at it. If you take property prices as they now stand, flood damage to a condominium in Florida will certainly be much more costly than the total destruction of some families' homes and farms in Bangladesh or the Maldive Islands. In fact, you could probably buy a large part of Bangladesh and all the Maldives for the price of a couple of small apartment blocks and a golf course in Palm Beach. But nowhere in the real world do they appear on the same set of accounts. Their relative value as real estate in money terms is meaningless outside an economics textbook. The only way to look at it that makes sense is to see their worth to their inhabitants.

We are examining a global problem but we don't have a global scale of value. We have only national scales based on national economies.

Most recognize at some point that the monetary values they are assigning in this way often bear little relation to the real world. Thus,

Fankhauser, at the end of a long calculation of the value of land around the world that might be lost to the sea, acknowledges: 'For many people, their homeland may be worth more than just its market value.' And at another point he says: 'It should be clear that the valuation of such damage aspects as human hardship will push economic valuation techniques to their limit, and quite possibly beyond.'

Measuring damage across the globe becomes still more muddled when what is being measured is not property but human life. Putting a price on human life is counter-intuitive. One's instinct is to say that it is beyond price. However, society does not in practice regard a human life as priceless. There is a limit to the amount that a government or community will spend to preserve one life. What this limit is varies with the circumstances, and the variation has very little logic behind it.

In the US, the Office of Management and Budget has estimated the number of people who might die from drinking water containing trihalomethane, and the cost of implementing a 1979 regulation limiting the amount that can be put in water. It came up with the figure of $200,000 for each life saved. This is bargain life-saving. The Environmental Protection Agency (EPA) decided that an 'acceptable risk' from a carcinogen is one chance in 10,000 of getting cancer for someone who has maximum exposure. This works out at $15 million per life saved, which the EPA takes as an average.

A person will not put a price on his life, but he will sometimes put a price on risking his life, engaging in an occupation that carries a certain risk and accepting danger money. The courts sometimes have to put a price on human life when they award compensation. This is based partly on a person's expected earning power, which makes sense if a family is being compensated for the loss of a bread-winner.

Estimates of the price that a government puts on a life come after the event. That is, they come from looking at how a government behaves and then making the calculation. Government agencies do not assign a value to lives and decide on this basis how to act. Nevertheless, there is always a competition for resources. If a health department considers introducing a new medical procedure, or initiating an inoculation programme, it does so according to the prevalence of the condition to be treated or prevented and its seriousness, in other words, how many people might die from it.

Fankhauser estimated the number of deaths that a doubling of carbon dioxide will cause, independent of deaths caused by storms or disease. Using the standard method, he costed the lives. He estimated that there will be 8775 deaths in the EU, at a value of $13,163 million in total, 6642 deaths in the US worth $9963 million, and 29,376 deaths in China – more than four times as many as in America – worth only $2938 million. As with property, so with lives. Death in China comes out costing a lot less than death in the Western world.

The valuation was made explicit in part of the IPCC Working Group 3 report, in Chapter 6, entitled *The Social Costs of Climate Change: Greenhouse Damage and the Benefits of Control*. Only this time someone noticed.

Costing damage expected from climate change, the authors assigned a value to statistical lives across the world. They valued a life in one of the OECD countries, the wealthy, developed countries, at $1.5 million. In middle-income countries they made it $300,000, and in the poorest countries $100,000. They admitted that few value-of-statistical-life studies have been done for developing world countries, so the last two figures are arbitrary, and also that the figure for developed countries was chosen from a wide range of possibilities. Given these qualifications, assigning different valuations for different societies makes economic sense. Willingness to pay implies ability to pay; it is no use someone being willing to pay money he or she does not have. Poor countries can afford to pay less for a life than wealthier countries.

Seven people wrote the chapter. The two lead authors have impeccable credentials. David Pearce is a British economist and environmentalist, director of the Centre for Economic and Social Research on the Global Environment, and a strong advocate of change to meet the environmental threat. The other author is Samuel Fankhauser, who now works for the Global Environment Facility.

The chapter passed through the peer review process without dispute, but it was spotted by a British environmental campaigner, Aubrey Meyer. Meyer runs the Global Commons Institute as a one-man band, with part-time help from a few like-minded people, from his house in north London, pouring out press releases and memos to delegates and button-holing ministers and officials. His basic contention, which is indicated in the name of his organization, is that the atmosphere is a global common and everyone has a right to an equal share in it. His ideas have had a considerable impact, either because of the zeal with which he propagates them or despite it, depending on who you talk to.

Meyer pounced on Chapter 6 of the report and decided that the authors were saying that an American or European life was worth more than an African's or an Asian's. This violated his idea of the global common. He raised this point in the press and with developing world delegations. In Britain, the newspaper *Independent on Sunday* took up his point and ran a front-page lead story headlined: 'One Western Life is Worth 15 in the Third World, says UN Report'. Other papers followed this up. Others joined Meyer in signing letters to newspapers. The authors of the IPCC report protested that they were not placing a real price on human lives, that the figures were merely an abstract economic valuation.

The Indian environment minister, Kamal Nath, invited Meyer to Delhi to address his department, then circulated to the environment ministers of other developing countries an angry objection to the report as it stood. 'It is impossible for us to accept that which is not ethically justifiable, technically accurate or politically conducive to the interests of poor people as well as the global common good', he wrote.

When Working Group 3 met in Geneva to finalize the report, Nath objected to it, saying, 'We unequivocally reject the valuation of life in Chapter 6'. He was followed by Chinese and Peruvians speaking in a similar vein. The Canadian chairman, Ken Bruce, tried to dismiss the objections saying the chapter had already been approved. 'This is the text. We all have planes to catch, we have to go home. The meeting is over', he declared. But the Cuban delegate and then the Brazilian insisted that they were down to speak and had objections that were still to be answered. Reluctantly, Bruce agreed to another meeting.

This took place in Montreal. Aubrey Meyer was present thanks to the last-minute gift of a plane ticket from a sympathizer. A lean, stringy figure darting around the conference hall, he made sure that developing world delegates heard his view. 'Look at the economists who wrote the report', he told them. 'Five of them are Americans or Europeans and the two Asians are attached to American institutions. You're getting a Western view of the value of life.'

The conference agreed under pressure to expunge the figures from the summary for policy-makers. The authors of the report protested that it had already been through the standard peer review process. None the less, the final text as amended simply gives different methods of assessing the value of life. The summary leaves out some of the argument and contains the cautionary words: 'There is no consensus about how to value statistical lives or how to aggregate statistical lives across countries. Monetary valuation should not obscure the human consequences of anthropogenic climate change damage, because the value of life has meaning beyond monetary considerations.'

This is a statement with which David Pearce would presumably agree. He himself wrote: 'The simplest procedure would be to value risks to life equally across the world on the grounds that we should be no less concerned with reducing risk in the developing world than in the developed world. This is not how the world actually behaves (think of foreign aid budgets), but as a moral principle it is a fair one.'[8]

None the less, he resented the interference with the report after it had passed through the normal procedures and resigned from the IPCC. 'This is a triumph of political correctness over scientific correctness', he said.

Meanwhile, climatic events are playing havoc with cost calculations. The first Conference of the Parties after Kyoto, which was supposed to tie up the loose ends of the agreement but failed to do so, was in Buenos Aires in November 1998. On its first day the conference passed a resolution expressing sympathy with the people of Central America in the wake of the hurricane disaster the previous month accompanying El Niño, the worst hurricane to hit the area in recorded history. The resolution said that this disaster 'demonstrates the need to take action to prevent and mitigate the effects of climate change.' The best estimates for El Niño-related weather damage around the world in the last three years puts the figure at $33 billion, and 21,000 deaths.

* * *

Meyer's argument was not simply an academic one about ethics; it related to policy. If the cost of lives is fed into a cost-benefit equation, and it can hardly be left out, then the value attached to developing world lives is important. If the value is low, then the cost-benefit analysis might show that the wealthy OECD countries should spend only a limited amount on slowing global warming and after that it was cheaper to deal with the consequences. If the developing world lives are valued as highly as OECD lives, then the cost of global warming becomes much greater.

Even on its own terms, cost-benefit analysis is a murky area ethically. Both the cost and the benefit in damage avoided are unequally distributed.

The no-regrets-and-no-more case is put by Frances Cairncross. She says the effects of climate change are uncertain, and that if there is to be severe damage it will probably not come for several decades: 'Adapting to climate change when that happens is undoubtedly the most rational course, for a number of reasons. . . Most countries will be richer then, and so able to build sea walls or drought-resistant plants . . . once climate change occurs, it will be clearer – as it is not now – what needs to be done and where.'[9]

But wait and see is not good policy for a number of reasons. One is that the less we reduce now, the more we will have to reduce in the future, and this will require a more rapid and therefore more difficult adjustment. Also, just as emitting CO_2 into the atmosphere has a delayed effect, so action to reduce emissions also has a delayed effect. We are now constructing the power plants, buildings and transport systems that will be warming the atmosphere several decades from now. If we are to build a different, climate-friendly infrastructure, we should be doing so now.

As much as the material infrastructure, people's mind-sets have a long lag-time. If carbon emissions are to be reduced, industry has to get used to the idea of finding ways to reduce them, by increasing efficiency and changing practices. Engineers, architects, designers and others must be motivated to look for new ways to do things. Energy efficiency will be increased and greenhouse gas emissions reduced by a combination of inventiveness and enthusiasm. Legislators must get used to reductions as an aim, so that they can discuss measures to promote it. Members of the public must get used to the idea of carbon efficiency, so that they will take it into account in their daily dealings and will accept public measures designed to promote it. This takes time. It is not a mind-set that can be switched on and off.

In this cost-benefit analysis, the benefit is in damage avoided. You calculate the benefit by calculating the damage, and this includes measures necessitated by the change in climate. The cost, on the other side of the equation, is the cost of reducing carbon emissions. But this is as questionable as the cost of damage. It depends on what improvements in efficiency we can make, what changes technology comes up with, and how lifestyles alter.

Nordhaus calculates the cost of mitigating climate change by assuming that present energy systems are the only ones in place, and that energy would have to be taxed to make people use less, and arrives at a figure of $200 billion a year. Again, this is extrapolating in a straight line. There is no reason to assume that we will continue to use energy in the same way or that we are using it in the most economical way now. There is plenty of reason to be optimistic about costs, and to believe that we can reduce the cost of energy. We don't know how far no-regrets measures can go. Most scientific bodies that have studied the subject believe we can make substantial economies in our use of energy at no extra cost. Some more carbon-efficient kinds of energy technology that now cost more may turn out to cost less when they are applied on a large scale and with major efforts to make them more efficient.

To set against any cost of reducing emissions, there are benefits that accrue, such as cleaner air, fewer traffic jams, and improved agriculture in certain sections. When economists factor in these, some say there may be a negative cost, ie a profit in shifting to a low-carbon economy.

Calculations of the future such as this are breath-taking in their assurance. William R Cline in his book *The Economics of Global Warming*, a key text for academics studying the subject, goes further than most. He calculates damage and cost up to the year 2300 and draws conclusions from this. What goods and services will constitute GNP 300 years from now? How usefully could someone in the year 1800 calculate the impact of events on the global economy today?

These calculations are sophisticated in their methods and precise in their conclusions, but they stand on flimsy foundations which consist of several layers of uncertainty. The costing is uncertain at the political-social level. How do you factor in the price of living in a more dangerous world, with more wars and more refugees? What will this do to defence budgets? Wars rarely have one cause but some of the effects of global warming in heavily populated areas will surely exacerbate existing tensions. The wars in the Horn of Africa and the genocide in Rwanda took place in areas of over-population and land shortage. How do you cost civil unrest? Or the pressures of unwanted immigration, or, for that matter, emigration? Or the disruption of world trade? Not to mention putting in the balance human happiness and suffering.

It is uncertain at the physical level. We don't know how far the growth and spread of plant pests will be stimulated, to ravage crops which might otherwise grow more rapidly. Sea level rise is highly uncertain. More storms are predicted, but not how many or where and what kind. If the damage caused by El Niño is to be attributed to climate change, it far exceeds in cost the price of reducing carbon. But the damage was mostly in Asia and central America.

The extent and pace of global warming is highly uncertain. The best the IPCC can come up with is that a doubling of carbon dioxide will lead to a temperature rise of between 1.5 degrees centigrade and 4.5 degrees centigrade, which is an uncertainty factor of 300 per cent. Our uncertainty does not end there. The climate could produce surprises. All these uncertainties interact and multiply. The coming together of climate change and other environmental problems will present an unprecedented situation.

Working Group 3 pointed to these uncertainties when it examined the literature on costs. It concluded: 'The IPCC does not endorse any particular range of values for the marginal damage of carbon dioxide emissions, but published estimates range between $5 and $125 per tonne of carbon emitted.' It then adds, in terms similar to those in the scientific section of the report: 'This range of estimates does not represent the full range of uncertainty.' It seems unnecessary to say after this, as the report does, 'Policy makers should not place too much confidence in the specific numerical results from any one analysis.'

These economists' precise conclusions are the result of mathematical calculation. They are calculating what can be calculated. They are setting numerical problems and getting numerical answers. But we should not confuse these with real-world answers.

It is quite legitimate to ask the questions they are asking. It would be irresponsible not to do so. Consideration of cost-benefit and of the price we may have to pay keeps us aware of our limitations. We cannot do everything. However, in asking the questions we should recognize that we don't have the answers.

Despite the mass of doubts, technical and social, interacting and multiplying, forecasts are still produced. But much forecasting, in this area as in others, is for psychological rather than practical reasons.

We human beings are afraid of the dark. With forecasts, we tell ourselves that we can shed some light in the darkness that is the unknown future. Predicting some particular tomorrow is an assurance that tomorrow will come.

This is seen at the public level in the fact that, although only a miniscule proportion of the population believes in astrology, popular newspapers and magazines all carry horoscopes and people read them. It is seen at the official level when committees produce cost forecasts on new technological projects with precision when really they are guessing, as is shown by the actual cost – for example Concorde, the Channel tunnel, and any number of military missile systems. Brokerage houses that advise agribusinesses hire meteorologists to produce weather forecasts for a particular week in the next growing season, although everyone knows these cannot be made with any accuracy. 'Our clients expect it of us', one broker said by way of explanation.

The Nobel Prize-winning economist Kenneth Arrow tells a story that illustrates the point. During World War Two, because of his knowledge of statistics, he was attached to a group of meteorologists in the US Air Force who were predicting the weather a month ahead. They concluded after a time that their forecasts were no more accurate than they would be if they relied on random chance. They reported this to their superiors, and suggested that they be assigned to some other duty that contributed usefully to the war effort. They received a reply that said: 'The Commanding General is well aware that the forecasts are no good. However, he needs them for planning purposes.'[10]

* * *

Some economists have even been bold enough to put a price on the nature that sustains us. Geoffrey Heal of Columbia University's

Business School and a team of colleagues have calculated that if industry had to perform all the work done by microbes and plants in cleansing, recycling and fertilizing, the bill would be over $30 trillion. In the real world as opposed to the abstract one of economics, this makes no more sense than putting a price on one's own life, or valuing a country in terms of its real estate. But it can be used as a reason for spending more money on preserving biodiversity, for those who like reasons to have numbers in them.

As human populations and activities spread, we are pushing out other species with which we share the planet. We are filling the world with things that are useful to us. Food crops have marched across the land, pushing out other plants. Sheep and cattle and poultry have undergone a population explosion at the expense of other animals. The biologist Edward O Wilson says: 'The one process going on now that will take millions of years to correct is the loss of species and genetic diversity by the destruction of natural habitats. This is the folly our descendants are least likely to forgive us.'[11]

Most environmentalists accept that species are becoming extinct at the rate of 30,000 a year. The United Nations Environment Programme reports that one-fourth of all mammal species and one-fifth of all bird species are in danger of extinction. A survey of 240,000 plant species by the World Conservation Union found that one in eight is at risk. But this is an area in which anyone can make up their own figures. No one knows how many species exist, let alone how many are becoming extinct. Some 1.4 million have been catalogued. Estimates by respected scientists of the total number range from 4 million to 20 million and more. Figures of extinction are arrived at by deduction and extrapolation, not observation. However, unlike most kinds of damage to the biosphere, extinction is final and irreversible. It would be well to apply the cautionary principle.[12]

Public attention is usually focused on picturesque animals which loom large in our imaginations, like the whale, the elephant and the tiger (although the inhabitants of rural Bengal may not worry about the reduction in tigers, which represent for them a constant danger). But these are less important for the continuing diversity of life than many micro-organisms and plants. Some of the extinctions are known and tabulated. Half the species of freshwater fish in Malaysia have died out in the last 50 years – that is half the species of fish, not just half the fish – 80 species of fish in Lake Victoria in East Africa, 21 species of bird in Hawaii.

Most species thrive in one kind of environment only, often only in one place. In 1978 the botanist Alwyn Gentry and a colleague found 38 species of plants that were found nowhere else in a forest area in Ecuador called the Centinela Ridge. When Gentry prepared to return for a further investigation, he found that the area had been cleared and planted with cacao and other crops.

Animals and plants, like a tribe of people, need a certain amount of space and a certain number of members below which they cannot survive as a group. As areas of natural habitat are reduced to islands in an ocean of towns, farms and roads, these become too small for some species to survive.

Species are also destroyed by an invasion of other species. This is a process that has been going on since the variety of life forms began, but it has been speeded up greatly in the past few centuries by people travelling the world and introducing species into areas where they have not been seen before, sometimes deliberately, sometimes inadvertently. The fish that have vanished from Lake Victoria are victims of the Nile perch, a fierce predator that was introduced into the lake by British settlers who wanted to fish it for sport. A Portuguese seaman shot the last dodo on the island of Mauritius in 1678, but it was not humans that brought about the dodo's extinction. The monkeys, dogs and pigs that men took to the island killed it off by eating its eggs. (The passing of the dodo provides an example of the interconnectedness of life forms and the unpredictable consequences of losing a species. The calvaria trees on Mauritius were dying out. An ingenious botanist worked out the reason; the tree's large, tough seeds had to pass through the gizzard of a big bird to germinate, and this function had been carried out by the dodo. Turkeys were imported and fed the seeds, and the calvaria trees have survived.)

Species die out because their environment changes, and this will happen as the world gets warmer. Plants, like animals, migrate with changing climate, that is, seeds and pollen will travel and succeeding generations will take root a little further on, but will do so slowly. Animals and plants may be prevented from migrating by man-made barriers such as towns, roads and cultivated land.

When we lose a species of plant, we lose a potential source of benefits to humanity. Most of the world's food comes from only 20 kinds of plant, with wheat, maize, rice and potatoes at the top. Yet thousands of species are edible, many of them undiscovered or untried. Many of our industrial materials – oils, fibres, dyes and gums – come from plants. Every month new and beneficial medicines are discovered which derive from plants. Fifty medicines in common use are derived from plants found in tropical rain forests, yet rain forests are being destroyed.

If several species of a plant exist, the plant is less vulnerable to disease, since some will resist a pest that destroys others. The Irish potato famine of the 1840s was devastating because the potatoes were genetically uniform and succumbed to the same blight. Today this could be countered by the introduction of new strains.

The gene pool is vital for another reason. Life forms are constantly evolving. Their evolution is measured in geological time rather than historical time, in millions of years rather than centuries. Extinctions curtail this evolution. They reduce the possibilities.

Finally, removing species is dangerous because we have learned to survive and flourish in the world as it is and we don't know how we will fare in one that is different. Micro-organisms play an essential part in functions that sustain ecosystems, such as cleaning and recirculating air and water, decomposing waste, pollinating crops and transporting nutrients. If we make too many changes, we may upset a complex mechanism. As the zoologist Richard Leakey writes: 'They represent the tangible elements of the stability and health that emerge from the entire biota of the Earth operating as a complex dynamic system. How exactly do health and stability emerge? We don't know. Can the system be reduced in size, through eliminating a proportion of a species in all ecological realms, and still be effective? We don't know. What are its most important components? We know this only incompletely.'[13]

The value of a varied plant gene pool has long been recognized, and gene banks have been established around the world from which plant breeders can draw. Samples of more than 500,000 seeds are held in gene banks operating under the rules of the International Plant Genetic Resources Institute. They do valuable work. Farming in Rwanda was restored quickly after the tribal slaughter in 1994 through the introduction of varieties of bean that had been previously collected in Rwanda and were stored in gene banks.

Even before the Convention on Biodiversity was presented to the 1992 Rio conference, environmentalists had impressed on governments that there was a problem there, and many joined in the establishment of protected areas, in which human activity is not allowed to interfere with the natural environment. These include tropical rain forests and jungle areas. Some of this land is open to tourists, some of it is lightly farmed. Eight per cent of the world's land area is protected in this way. Much of this is in developing countries, paid for by the Western world. Debt-for-nature swaps, in which a Western government agrees to forego a debt by a developing country in exchange for preserving a rain forest, is a common form that this takes. The countries poorest in material wealth are usually those that are richest in species.

The Convention is a weak treaty; it makes recommendations, but it imposes few specific obligations on signatories, and leaves open large areas to be negotiated. It says all parties should be given access to developments in biotechnology. In a paragraph intended to favour developing world countries it says cautiously that access to species should be on preferential terms 'where mutually agreed'. It also says this should be 'consistent with the adequate and effective protection of intellectual property rights'. Western pharmaceutical companies are arguing with developing world countries over the sharing of profits from medicines they derive from plants in those countries.

Over the objections of the Americans, the negotiators of the convention included provisions on safety in biotechnology research. They call for new regulations on safety in research with genetically modified organisms, as recommended by a panel of scientists. A dissenting minority said there is no reason to make a distinction between genetically modified organisms and those created by traditional breeding methods.

American pharmaceutical and biotechnology companies worried about the possibilities of regulation implied in some of its clauses, and so did the American Farm Bureau and the big cattle ranchers. At their urging, President Bush refused to sign the convention. Clinton signed it but the Senate, subjected to fierce lobbying, has refused to ratify it.

Natural habitats will be preserved if it pays people to preserve them. In Africa large areas have been turned into animal reserves which become tourist attractions with jobs for local people. In El Salvador, the government has launched a scheme, with help from the British Natural History Museum, to subsidize coffee-farmers if their farms preserve biodiversity. Some pharmaceutical companies have reached bio-prospecting agreements with developing world countries which preserve natural habitats and give the company the right to prospect there for plants that may be useful. However, progress is being held up by arguments over who owns the rights to seeds that may be genetically modified, perhaps seeds that have been cultivated for medicinal purposes for years.

Now we come back to economics. Three scientists based at Cambridge University have drawn up a plan for doubling the protected areas over a period of years which they believe will preserve 90 per cent of the species that are now being lost, and they have costed it.[14] Andrew Balmford of the university's Conservation Biology Group says: 'We don't know exactly what we're losing but we know we're losing a lot. The usual response is that we can't afford to conserve all this. But compared to the value of what we're losing, the cost is small, and certainly affordable.'

The scientists' recommendations for reserved areas are similar to those of others who have studied the subject. The areas do not have to be unpopulated but human activity should be low-impact. Where there are farms they would preserve hedgerows, use very little pesticides, keep the stubble and leave land fallow for a season. Forests could be cropped; bio-research could be undertaken providing only samples of plants were removed, which is the usual practice.

Currently, $6 billion a year is being spent on protected areas. The scientists calculate that a representative 15 per cent of the world's surface with different kinds of habitat could be protected for another $16.6 billion a year (including one-off purchases the cost of which would be amortized). They then point to other measures designed to protect biodiversity in agriculture, fisheries and other areas, which would cost $300 billion a year. Nature reserves, they say, are 'a remarkable bargain'. They would like the money to come from phasing out subsidies that damage the environment.

All this would be consistent with the Biodiversity Convention, which calls for extended protection of this kind, and also calls for the developed countries to bear the cost. Its main virtue is not economic; it suggests that as people spread out yet further around the world, the extinction of other species is not inevitable or unstoppable.

CHAPTER **6**

SOME MORE
NITTY-GRITTY

Foreign policy demands scarcely any of those qualities which are peculiar to a democracy; on the contrary, it calls for the perfect use of all those qualities in which a democracy is deficient. Democracy is favourable to the increase of the internal resources of a state; it diffuses wealth and comfort, and fortifies the respect for law in all classes of society, but it can only with great difficulty regulate the details of an important undertaking, persevere in a fixed design, and work out its execution in spite of serious obstacles – Alexis de Toqueville[1]

MOST OF THE unanswered questions concerning the Kyoto agreement are still unanswered and will have to be thrashed out in the years ahead. Some will be worked out during the implementation.

The first Conference of the Parties after Kyoto, COP 4 in Buenos Aires, did little to advance the process. After what seems like the inevitable all-night meetings and last-minute decisions, the best the delegates could do was to draw up a plan of action and set up subsidiary bodies to work out details. Some delegates dubbed this the Mañana Mandate.

The conference decided to continue the pilot phase of Activities Implemented Jointly, or AIJ, which means rich countries reducing emissions in poorer countries, and it set up a review process to draw conclusions. They found that AIJ followed the biblical prophecy 'To everyone that hath shall be given'. Most of the projects had been set up in countries which already attract a lot of foreign investment. Representatives of countries that had been neglected pointed out that only 6 of the 95 projects were in East Asia and only one was in Africa. It was agreed that these areas should get more.

During the conference, President Menem said Argentina would make a voluntary commitment to reduce emissions. American delegates, mindful of the Senate's insistence that developing countries must participate before it would ratify the Kyoto Protocol, were eager to ensure that this was reported in the US press.

An independent body is to be set up to monitor emissions, so that governments will not have their own assessments taken at face value. Even so, there will be room for doubt. In calculating emissions of carbon by adding up the fossil fuel that is burned, there is an uncertainty factor of 10 per cent. With methane, which comes from many sources, it is 30 per cent. At Buenos Aires, Australia revised its account of 1990 emissions downward by 50 per cent. The United States revised its account of carbon absorbed through land use changes upward by nearly 100 per cent. The next Conference of the Parties took place in Bonn in November 1999, and it did not bring mañana much closer. The EU called for ratification by all the industrialized countries by 2002. There were even fewer decisions reached than at Buenos Aires and the arguments remained unresolved.

President Clinton signed the Kyoto Protocol during the Buenos Aires conference but the Senate shows no sign of ratifying it, despite the baking sidewalks outside the Capitol and the record high temperatures in Washington in summertime. The protocol is a victim to the belief of America's founding fathers in the system of checks and balances in government. The president conducts foreign policy but only the Senate can ratify a treaty and it must do so by a two-thirds majority.

Sir Crispin Tickell, after a long career as a diplomat, may say that governments do not like international disapproval and do not like vetoing UN decisions. But Senators do not have to deal with foreign governments or face their disapproval. They have to deal with their constituents, who are used to their four-wheel drive vehicles and multiple appliances and their bountiful supplies of cheap energy. They also have to deal with corporations in the fuel and automobile industries, and with the corporations and the people who fund their election campaigns.

Monitoring joint implementation projects encounters another difficulty, and this will apply to much of the Clean Development Mechanism: its basis is counter-factual. If a country builds an efficient gas-fired power station in place of the inefficient coal-fired plant that would have been built there otherwise, it reduces carbon emissions. But who can say by how much? Who can say how inefficient the other plant would have been? A government supplies solar power to a group of developing world villages, thus saving trees that would otherwise have been cut down for firewood. This is a boon for the villagers. The women do not have to gather wood as fuel, denuding the local forests, and this saves carbon. There are health benefits also. It saves them from literally back-breaking work, and it saves families from the effects on their lungs of burning wood in a small, enclosed space, one of the most common causes of disease in much of the developing world. But how much wood would they have gathered if they did not have the solar power? How many trees were saved? Who can decide this? All this has still to be worked out.

The Clean Development Mechanism and the quota trading are the flexible mechanisms – the 'flex-mex' – with which the US hopes to make it easier for itself to meet their Kyoto obligations. But the Americans also seem to be flexible in their use of language. The protocol said these mechanisms were to be 'supplemental' to domestic reductions in emissions. This was deliberately left undefined, but to most other delegates at Kyoto it meant that they must be the minor part, with the major part being reducing emissions at home. The US Administration is assuming that flex-mex can be as large as it wants and the term 'supplemental' can mean anything it wants it to mean. 'So why use the word "supplemental" if it doesn't mean anything?' one European demanded, at one of the post-Buenos Aires meetings.

If flex-mex is to be totally flexible, with no limit on trading and credits under the Clean Development Mechanism, then Western countries could make all of their reductions in other countries, with many of them being phantom reductions. They would buy the quotas possessed by Russia and the Ukraine because these two countries are now emitting much less carbon than they did in 1990. These are the emission quotas known as hot air. Other countries of the former Soviet Union may join in this. Kazakhstan recently agreed to accept the Kyoto terms, which is no sacrifice because it has emission quotas to sell.

With no limits at all on flex-mex, the US could pour 20 per cent more carbon into the atmosphere than it did in 1990, and Japan 10 per cent more, buying reduction quotas to fulfull their obligations. They would be meeting the letter of the Kyoto Protocol but not the spirit. This would be bad news. The Kyoto Protocol with all its limitations is only a small first step in the process of reducing our impact on the climate, and is of value only if it is a part of a long-term process. This process will mean changing some of the technologies by which we live, and shifting to ones that produce less carbon and less of the other greenhouse gases.

If the world's leading industrialized power and leading emitter of carbon were to take no important steps towards changing its ways, and achieved a reduction in greenhouse gas emissions only by tricky accountancy, this would be a poor example. It would not provide the leadership that might induce developing countries to join in the process at the next stage. Nor would it do much to stimulate the advances in technology which will make it easier to reduce carbon emissions.

The European Union has already apportioned its target of an aggregate 8 per cent drop below 1990 levels by 2008–2012 among its members. Britain is due to have 12.5 per cent less; Environment Minister John Prescott believes it can be down to 20 per cent less. Germany and Denmark are due to be down by 21 per cent. These are the big cuts. All of these countries have already reduced emissions, Britain because of the move from coal to gas, Germany because it has shut down inefficient East German industries and also taken carbon-saving measures, and Denmark because of an expansion of wind power. Most others have lesser reductions to achieve but the five poorest countries are allowed increases in carbon emissions as they expand their industry.

Reaching the Kyoto targets is likely to be more difficult to achieve in Europe than in America and Japan. For one thing, America uses more coal, the most carbon-intensive fuel, and can cut more easily by switching away from coal. Also, 20 per cent of America's greenhouse gases are methane and nitrous oxide, which are going down anyway because of clean air legislation, and these are only 14 per cent of Europe's.

The Western countries will achieve some of their targets by flex-mex. Without it, the US would have to reduce its emissions by nearly 30 per cent in the next decade to reach its target, and the EU would have to reduce by 25 per cent. In trying to reduce carbon emissions, we are running up a down escalator.

Aircraft are contributing 3.5 per cent of the warming of the planet, emitting carbon and also nitrous oxide which, in the stratosphere, produces as much warming effect as carbon. Air travel is increasing at the rate of 5 per cent a year. The IPCC produced a special report on aviation in 1999. As well as emitting greenhouse gases, aircraft help to create low-altitude cirrus clouds, which have a warming effect, although, as the IPCC says, in terms which are now familiar, 'the mechanisms associated with increases in cloud cover are not well understood and need further investigation'. Supersonic planes, flying five miles higher than subsonic aircraft, have a warming effect five times greater than subsonic planes. Most of these are military – the British and French Concordes are the only supersonic airliners – and they are relatively few in number.

Emissions by aircraft are constantly being reduced due to improvements in fuel-efficiency. Airliners are now 70 per cent more fuel efficient than they were 40 years ago; the Boeing 777 uses half as much fuel per passenger-mile as the 727. There is plenty of incentive to improve fuel efficiency since fuel is typically one-third of the operating cost of an airline. Engines that reduce nitrous oxide emissions by 40 per cent are technically feasible. The IPCC suggests a number of measures to encourage these developments, such as taxes and reducing certain subsidies. Most of these will add to the price of air travel.

European governments are all taking steps to reduce their carbon emissions. The principal method used is taxes and subsidies to provide the stick and carrot.

In Britain the government is introducing a Climate Change Levy, taxing industry according to the amount of energy used, raising taxes on petrol on a sliding scale, and recycling the revenues to business so that there is no net increase in taxation. It will apply to coal and natural gas, and is structured so as to encourage energy efficiency and the use of renwables, ie non-fossil fuels. Germany has an energy tax which goes to subsidize renewable energy. As a result, Germany has more than 2000 megawatts of wind power, enough to supply electricity to two million people, and 10,000 new jobs have been created. The four Scandinavian countries and The Netherlands all have a carbon tax, albeit with important exemptions designed to ensure the international competitiveness of their industries. The Netherlands has had for some time an integrated plan to reduce energy use including town planning, transport, industrial and taxation policy. Japan is also taking measures. The Japanese government installed 70,000 solar power systems in homes with heavy subsidies, and Japan alone is increasing its nuclear power programme.

Britain and Germany are on course to meet their Kyoto emissions targets, with Britain heading for its more ambitious reductions, but the EU as a whole is not. The European Commission has proposed a series of measures, including a harmonized energy tax and a continent-wide emission trading scheme.

The US Administration is taking steps to reduce carbon emissions. The Green Lights programme includes subsidies and tax credits for alternatives to fossil fuels, principally solar power; stepped-up research into alternatives; and incentives for reforestation. These are all soft measures. Legislation in recent years has had an effect, although some of it was designed for other environmental purposes. The Corporate Average Fuel Efficiency Bill (CAFE), passed in 1973 in the wake of the sudden increase in the price of Middle East oil, resulted in a doubling of the fuel efficiency of American cars. The intention of this was to reduce urban pollution, not to reduce carbon emissions, but this was one effect.

Administration efforts to raise further efficiency requirements for cars and buildings were opposed vigorously by the automobile and construction industries respectively, and thwarted by Congress. But the US Administration is planning other measures, and the Senate is coming around. A group of Senators recently called for regulations to increase the fuel efficiency of cars.

In America, taxation is not the principal instrument for reducing emissions. A proposal for an energy tax was shot down by Congress in 1993. Congress has steadfastly refused to increase the tax on petrol, which is the cheapest in the world. Americans may tell opinion pollsters that they want their government to take steps on climate change, but they don't want to drive their cars less. The instrument the Administration hopes to use is a cap on the emissions allowed accompanied by a scheme for tradeable quotas, similar to the one in place for sulphur emissions. It uses the market mechanism which makes it more palatable to American business than other measures. As envisaged, the scheme would operate internationally; American corporations could buy emission quotas from other countries as a part of the national effort to meet its target.

Industry is coming around to the idea. Three major corporations, General Motors, British Petroleum and Monsanto, recently joined with the World Resources Institute to press for carbon reductions through 'flexible and market-oriented policies'. The Business Council of America says it would accept such a scheme providing it were international.

Senator Joseph Lieberman, a Democrat from Connecticut, wants to encourage tradeable quotas by allowing corporations to get credit for reducing emissions now. Along with four other Senators, he has introduced a bill in the Senate authorizing the president to give credit to any company that reduces its emission of greenhouse gases now against any regulatory requirements enacted in the next ten years. The bill also specifies that these credits can be sold or traded.

Senator Bob Kerrey of Nebraska wants farmers to be able to claim payment for carbon they have taken out of the atmosphere, either by planting crops for that purpose or for switching to tilling methods that fix carbon in the soil. He has introduced a bill to give farmers credit for sequestering carbon in advance of the setting up of a trading system. The main meeting room in his suite of offices in the Senate Office Building is decorated with two crossed spades on the wall, to remind him of his farming constituents' concerns.

A one-time pharmacist and successful entrepreneur, Kerrey harks back to his college science lessons when he explains how farmers can sequester carbon, or turn crops into biomass to be used again as fuel: 'You can have low-till or no-till farming, in which the ground is not turned over but the seeds are pushed into the soil with machines . . . This sequesters carbon without releasing more into the air. It's particularly suitable for wheat, soy beans and corn. If industry can get credits which they can sell for not emitting carbon, then farmers should be able to get credits for sequestering carbon which they can sell. We want a level playing field.'

Preliminary trading in carbon emissions is going on already. Carlton Bertel is a member of the brokerage firm of Cantor Fitzgerald, and the head of the firm's ten-person department that trades in sulphur emission credits. His office is on the 125th floor of the World Trade Center, at the foot of Manhattan. From this height he can look down the length of Manhattan Island and across the two rivers that are its boundaries. There is still sulphur in the urban air, and on hot, humid summer days as he looks out of his window the haze is tinted with yellow, so that he looks down on the scene through a pale yellow filter. The haze used to be a deeper shade of yellow, and over the years he has been able to see the success of the anti-pollution measures as the sulphur colour becomes fainter.

An environmental consultant before he became a broker in this field, Bertel is trading now in options on carbon quotas. 'Electrical utilities and gas companies are buying options on carbon emission permits at a few cents a ton of carbon now . . . They reckon it's going to come, and they already have some experience of trading in sulphur emissions. They want to be first in the field to buy quota points when it happens. As demands firm up and as a trading system gets closer, the price will rise, of course.'

Europeans also believe that international emissions trading will come in. In Britain the Department of the Environment has organized meetings with industry groups to prepare them for the time when they will be trading reductions in carbon emissions with other countries. The City has shown an interest, and the London Futures Exchange, the London-based International Petroleum Exchange and the Frankfurt Stock Exchange are all bidding to run the market in emission quotas.

* * *

Developing countries are increasing their emissions faster than the industrialized countries. They are expanding their industries and, being less technologically sophisticated, they are less energy efficient and produce more carbon per unit of production. In America, 8 per cent of electric power is lost in transmission, in Japan 7 per cent. In India and Pakistan the figures are 22 and 28 per cent. In developing countries, most cars and trucks are old and infirm and run on bad roads, and they are 20 to 50 per cent less fuel-efficient. A country becomes more efficient as it becomes wealthier.

At present, the industrialized countries are still the biggest emitters. China produces 638 million tonnes of carbon in 1998, compared with America's 1456, although China has nearly four times the population. But developing countries' emissions will increase as they expand their industrial production. Emissions by the industrialized countries have about doubled since 1950; those of the developing countries have almost quadrupled. Among the biggest developing countries, India's emissions have increased by 75 per cent in the last decade, Indonesia's by 80 per cent and Brazil's by 40 per cent.

The pattern of the world economy indicates that this trend will continue, as many poorer countries develop and manufacturing industry leaves the wealthy countries for the developing world. On present trends, non-OECD countries will be the biggest emitters of carbon by 2050. In most of the developing world, reducing emissions also means running up a down escalator as the escalator is moving even faster.

In the long run, over the next century or so, and serious thinking about climate change must be in this sort of time span, it is what these countries do that will count most, not what the West does.

Yet we cannot tell them not to develop their industries any more than we can tell them not to build refrigerators because of their effect on the ozone layer. There is no doubt about what the people in these countries want. It is what they see on their television sets and cinema screens, the Western affluent society, and the society they see pictured is even more affluent than the real one. We can tell them about the growing inequities and discontent and social fracture that our consumer society has brought. We can deplore materialism and the manufactured dissatisfaction that is the engine of the consumer society. Here and there, and even in the developing world, there are those who preach the virtues of a simpler lifestyle than our present one, on a more human scale. But these are a small minority, and the number who practise what they preach is smaller still.

For the moment, the creators of incessant demand and dissatisfaction have won. The consumer society is the model to which non-Westerners aspire. They want cars, they want air travel, they want modern kitchens, they want smart clothes, they want a diet rich in meat. And they want electricity.

Electricity is not an efficient way of using power. Power has to be used to drive a turbine that will create an electric current and the electricity is then transmitted along wires (the exception is the photovoltaic cell, which creates electricity directly). Energy is lost at each stage. Only 3 per cent of the energy used to drive the turbine comes out of an ordinary incandescent electric light bulb. But electricity is the most convenient form of power for a consumer, able to summon it up with the flick of a switch. Everybody wants it. Since 1970 the growth in electricity has been twice the growth in energy use.

Two billion people in the world are without electricity, according to the World Bank. On present growth rates, Asia will have 1,150,000 megawatts more electric generating capacity 20 years from now. That is one-third of the entire world's capacity today. This will require fuel. Today most of the fuel to drive turbines to produce electricity is coal.

Developing countries are not only inefficient in their use of fuel; their industries are also carbon-intensive. The OECD countries, the wealthy countries, in the aggregate get 37 per cent of their electricity from coal, the most carbon-intensive fuel, and 25 per cent from natural gas. They get 24 per cent from nuclear power and 15 per cent from hydro power, which produce no carbon. China with 1.2 billion people, and India with 780 million, both get more than 70 per cent of their electricity from coal. Both these countries have huge coal reserves; China is second only to the US as a coal producer.

They have more pressing problems than climate change, such as disease, malnutrition and overcrowding. Millions of people die in developing countries from diseases that are preventable by public health measures, such as the provision of clean water. Development is their top priority. Not that those countries are unconcerned about pollution. According to the World Health Organization, the most polluted air in the world is in the big cities in the developing countries, cities like Beijing, Shanghai, Calcutta, Mexico City, Delhi. Any visitor to one of these cities has experienced the fumes from the two-stroke motors of the taxi-rickshaws that put-put around the streets and the belching black smoke from the abused engines of old trucks and cars, not to mention the smells from sewage. It is a rough-and-ready rule that rich people create global environmental problems, poor people local environmental problems.

Developing countries are more vulnerable to climate change. A warmer climate in India means drought, which could turn some of its productive food areas near the centre of the continent into desert. One-tenth of China's territory containing two-thirds of its population is below the flood level of major rivers. The most populous part of Bangladesh is barely above sea level. One-third of Egypt's arable land is in the Nile Delta, three feet above sea level. All developing countries are more directly dependent on food production than industrialized countries.

These countries will also suffer more because they are poorer. They are less able to prevent climate damage, by changing crops or building sea walls, for instance. They are also less able to cope with the consequences. A farmer in East Anglia or Kansas may go on the dole if his farm is wiped out by the enroaching sea or by drought. If he can salvage some money he might buy a farm somewhere else. A farmer in central Africa will starve or head for a refugee camp.

Developing countries have always been suspicious that Western suggestions that they might have to change their development path are aimed at curtailing their growth, which is not surprising given the background of Western economic domination. A Chinese scientist who was a delegate to the preliminary conferences inserted into several of his speeches his recollection of walking through a Chinese city as a child and seeing a cemetery for Europeans with a sign outside saying 'No Chinese Allowed'. He would conclude the story by declaring, 'Now no one will decide China's future but ourselves!'

The nearest spokesmen for developing countries have come to agreeing to participate in efforts to reduce greenhouse gas emissions has been to talk occasionally about the aim of convergence, the West's emissions coming down as the developing world's rises until they are the same per capita. This accords with abstract logic and it is acceptable as an ultimate aim, like world peace. It is not practical politics. For a Western country to reduce its carbon emissions to anything like those that a country such as India can achieve in the predictable future would be to accept unimaginable poverty.

It has always been clear that the world cannot sustain six billion-plus people with the consumption levels of the Western world today, building the same kind of buildings, driving the same number of cars, eating the same kind of food, throwing away the same amount of garbage. Some of the limits are worryingly close. China on present form will have the GNP per capita of Taiwan by 2030. If

1.2 billion Chinese then consume grain at the rate of the Taiwanese today, this will leave a shortfall of 400 million tonnes, to be made up by imports. Total world exports of grain today are 200 million tonnes. As it is, China feeds 22 per cent of the world's population with a steadily improving diet on 7 per cent of the world's arable land. Much of our grain is raised to feed cattle; it takes four times as much grain to create a given amount of protein in cattle as it does if it were used as vegetable. As people become wealthier, they want more meat. As the Chinese acquire a higher standard of living, they will compete on the world market for raw materials, and drive up prices. The carbon problem is another limitation, another reason why they cannot go the same way.

On carbon emissions, China has always been regarded as the biggest threat. It is the biggest country in population and the biggest coal producer, expanding its industries rapidly, with an annual economic growth rate hovering around 7 per cent. And China has refused to have anything to do with commitments on reducing emissions. Senator Chuck Hagel confronted the chief Chinese delegate at the Kyoto conference and demanded, 'Won't you ever agree to commitments to reduce?' and the Chinese retorted, 'No, no, never! Not for fifty years'. This was an off-the-cuff retort rather than a policy statement but it is an indicator of official resistance.

Other developing countries are also getting more interested in low-carbon or no-carbon means of producing energy even while adopting a stand-offish approach to the Kyoto Protocol. India, with coal reserves second only to the US and China, has a ministry for renewable energy and is one of the world leaders in wind power, with more than 900 megawatts of wind power generating capacity. The government subsidizes the manufacture of wind turbines. India has no shortage of fuel but transporting coal across large distances by rail is expensive.

Perhaps it was with all this in mind that the director of the UN Development Programme, James Speth, confronted with the US Senate's demand that developing countries participate meaningfully in climate change measures, insisted, 'Developing countries *are* participating meaningfully'.

The developing countries will continue to develop. We cannot tell them that they must forgo hopes of Western-style prosperity in order to save the climate. We can only work out, along with the developing countries themselves, ways for them to develop along different lines. José Goldemberg, a Brazilian physicist and former minister of the environment, says: 'Developing countries have a fundamental choice. They can mimic the industrialized nations and go through an economic development phase that is dirty, wasteful and creates an enormous legacy of environmental pollution, or they can leapfrog . . . and incorporate modern and efficient technologies.'[2]

Most of these modern and efficient technologies that can perform a leapfrog will come from the West. Some official Western aid is channelled into climate-friendly channels. The World Bank now has a Solar Initiative, to promote renewable energy – solar and other kinds – in developing countries, and this finances renewable energy projects. It finances the Photovoltaic Market Transformation Initiative: low interest loans to manufacturers. It finances wind farms in India, mini-hydro and solar energy programmes in Sri Lanka.

Most technology is owned by private corporations. These are involved in foreign aid programmes, and in the Global Environment Facility (GEF) and joint implementation projects. The Kyoto Protocol specifically says that private organizations as well as governments can be partners in joint ventures. Developing countries accept this; any ideological reservations are swept away by the sense that in today's world, free enterprise capitalism is the only game in town. But they want what they call 'horizontal' transfer. This means that knowledge and methods are transferred so that local communities can operate them.

Corporations tend to promote vertical transfer, in which technology is controlled by the corporation. As Tim Forsyth, an economist who has looked at technological transfer and climate control, wrote: 'If the clean development mechanism effectively subsidizes exports from industrialized countries, it will result in increased adoption of Northern technologies and a decreased competitiveness of Southern technology producers . . . and lead to a dependence on imported technologies that are not as appropriate to developing societies as those developed locally.'[3]

They will not be able to consume materials and throw away materials at the same rate as we in the West have been doing, but neither will we. Our societies will also come up against limits to growth. If we want to continue to have a rising standard of living, we will have to find different ways to achieve more comfort, more leisure, more enjoyment, and the developing countries will as well.

* * *

Now here is some good news. Carbon emissions worldwide are no longer rising. The IPCC's projected business-as-usual trend is not happening.

When the last major IPCC report was published, in 1995, global emissions of carbon dioxide were increasing at the rate of 2 per cent a year. Since then they have levelled off and in 1998, according to Worldwatch, the respected American environmental organization, they fell by 0.5 per cent. Worldwatch says: 'The decline in emissions stems partly from improved energy efficiency and from falling coal use, spurred by new efficiency standards and the removal of energy subsidies.'

Most importantly, this is not accompanied by a decline in economic activity. The world economy grew by almost 2.8 per cent in 1998. In both Europe and America, emissions levelled off, rising at less than 1 per cent, while economies continued to grow.

Energy use and carbon emissions are being decoupled from economic growth. This refutes the arguments of those who say that cutting back on carbon must damage the economy.

This is a change in the right direction. The great supertanker of energy use is beginning to turn. The reduction in emissions is not enough, or anywhere near it. The present rate of greenhouse gas emissions is what is changing the climate. If the process is to be slowed, or even halted, we will have to reduce that rate, eventually by 60 per cent if we are going to stop the change, according to the first IPCC report.

Now here is some very good news. China's carbon emissions are no longer rising, but are falling. China's emissions rose by 28 per cent between 1990 and 1997. But in 1997 its emissions dropped slightly, and in 1998 they fell by 3.9 per cent. This is despite the fact that its economy continues to expand, and its GNP increased by 7.2 per cent in 1998. China also has broken the link between rising carbon emissions and rising GNP. This shows other developing countries that they can become richer without emitting more greenhouse gases.

It has not done this as its contribution to a global effort to reduce carbon. It has refused to have anything to do with global efforts. It has done more to reduce emissions than any of the countries that signed the Kyoto Protocol, but its motivation was economic. China does not subscribe to the Clean Development Mechanism, which would mean cooperating with the West to reduce climate change. But the State Planning Committee has listed 15 items of technology for improving energy efficiency and reducing urban pollution with which China would like help. Every one of them is relevant to reducing carbon emissions. They include fuel cells as a substitute for petrol or oil-burning motors, gasification, combined cycle power systems and forest management.

An American official said, 'We talk to the Chinese about technology transfer, and they're interested. But we don't talk about climate change. If we do that we don't get anywhere. We talk about improving industrial efficiency, about saving money.'

The Chinese government has given a high priority to increasing energy efficiency. It has held the growth in energy consumption to half the growth in its economy, in contrast to every other developing country, where energy consumption has risen proportionately to economic growth. It now gets twice as much output per unit of energy as it did 20 years ago. It has created a national fund to invest in energy efficiency, and its own Green Lights programme, encouraging, for instance, the use of high-efficiency light bulbs. With World Bank funding, it has developed efficiency management companies, which show enterprises how to improve energy efficiency and take a share of the savings.

The Chinese authorities estimated that urban pollution has caused three million deaths in ten years. Although coal is still the principal form of industrial energy, the government has slashed the annual subsidy to coal, and household heating in the cities is being changed from coal to natural gas. The government is also tackling the toxic pollution of rivers by industry and the over-use of chemical fertilizers in farming with new regulations and new efforts at enforcement. It is stepping up its programme of removing sulphur and nitrogen from its coal-burning power plants and closing down less efficient smaller plants. Also, in contrast once again to most other developing countries, China has kept down its population. This is probably the most important single factor in economic success or failure in a developing country.

The treaty, the contractual path, is one road ahead. If the Kyoto Protocol is ratified and the terms are fulfilled, this will open the way for negotiating further reductions in carbon emissions which will include the developing countries, and all countries will start re-directing their growth. This would be the most desirable outcome. The Kyoto Protocol has many flaws. It is vague on some points, it makes few serious demands, and it allows Western countries to limit themselves to cosmetic reductions. Most importantly, it will go only a little way to meeting the problem. The Battelle Laboratory, a leading American think tank, calculates that if all its conditions are met, it will still only delay the build-up of greenhouse gases by eight years. However, it is the first definite step along the road of international agreement and the only step on this particular path. If we don't take it, we will have to find another path ahead.

Two things will influence the pace at which we move. One is the public appreciation of the situation, which depends on the messages from the scientists and the politicians and, more than anything else, the behaviour of the climate. More El Niños bringing death and destruction in Asia and Central America will provide a push. Since most of us are selfish, storms and droughts and other climatic events which damage Western countries will provide a bigger one.

The pull will come from new ideas and new technology which will make it easier to reduce greenhouse gas emissions. This will determine how easy and comfortable it is to switch to new forms of power generation, whether industry finds it profitable to pursue this course, and whether tangible benefits will come from new technologies and new ways of doing things.

CHAPTER 7

NEW WAYS OF DOING THINGS

*Limiting carbon emissions is not primarily a matter of economic cost,
but of culture, institutions, and politics in the broadest sense –*
Michael Grubb[1]

*The automobile has changed our dress, manners, social customs,
vacation habits, the shape of our cities, consumer purchasing patterns
and positions in intercourse –* John Cresswell Keats[2]

SOME 200 MILES west of Denver, Colorado,
7100 feet high in the Rocky Mountains, stands the headquarters
of the Rocky Mountain Institute, an organization dedicated to
the efficient and socially beneficial use of energy. It is a stone and
glass building in a serpentine shape, with solar panels at a 45-degree
angle on the flat roof. The only fuel it uses is a small amount of
wood in two small stoves, which are mainly decorative. Ninety-
nine per cent of the heat comes from the sun, captured and con-
served by the solar panels and the architecture of the building.
Workers in their shirtsleeves may look out on snow on the mountain-

side where the temperature is well below freezing, or else down a corridor to where bananas, oranges and mangoes grow.

From the Rocky Mountains, you can look up on a wide sky that is often clear and blue even on the coldest days. But the terraced houses in a narrow street in the London suburb of Richmond lie under a sky that is often cloudy and grey, and there is no wide expanse above. None the less, even on grey days when the sunlight is filtered through clouds, one of the houses in Raleigh Road gets nearly all the energy it needs for its electric lighting and household appliances from the sun. The energy is delivered through photo-voltaic (PV) cells which constitute half the roof tiles. They are coated with a thin grey translucent material, so that they look little different from the slate tiles.

The Rocky Mountain Institute's lighting and heating come virtually free, for the extra capital cost paid for itself in bills saved in the first year. The lighting bills at the house in Richmond are slightly higher than they would be for conventional electricity, but the price will come down as more PV roof tiles are produced and sold and economies of scale come into play. Even now, a Scottish farmhouse three miles from the electric grid has installed PV roof tiles to produce its electricity because it is cheaper than linking up to the grid.

The Richmond house burns no fuel and no carbon is produced to light its lamps. It is owned by Solar Century, a company started by Jeremy Leggett. He was an oil industry consultant until he came to feel that he was, as he says, 'quite literally fuelling a threat to the future'. He switched sides to become the chief scientist of Green-peace. Leggett is a familiar figure at climate change conferences, where his zealous partisanship and grasp of the science make him a formidable debater. Now he tries to persuade the world of the potentiality in solar power. 'The solar revolution is coming', he says. 'It is now inevitable. The only question left unanswered is, will it come in time?'

The technology for moving to low-carbon energy, and slowing or halting global warming, is here or is under development. Using it means changing our way of thinking.

A massive report by UNEP, *Global Environment Outlook 2000*, dealing with an array of environmental issues, concludes that current policies are unsustainable. But it also says: 'The results [of several studies] confirm that in principle, the knowledge and technological base to solve environmental issues are available, and that if these alternative policies were implemented immediately and pursued with vigour, they could indeed set the world on a more sustainable course.'[3]

The executive director of UNEP, Klaus Töpfer, drew a stark conclusion from this in an address in London presenting the report: 'The developed world has the technology to bring about the fundamental changes needed to save millions of people from hunger, thirst and ill-health. But there is no incentive to apply it because politicians are not forcing manufacturers to do so.'

So the crucial question is not what we can do but how hard we try. There is much that we can do right now.

We – meaning us and our governments – can do more to cost externalities, the price of a product that is external to the production process. This is something we as a society have learned to do in the last few years. We now cost the smoke an industrial plant pours into the atmosphere and the sewage it puts into the river. We know now that air and water do not come free. This kind of accounting is still at an early stage. Calculating the entire cost of a product, from the effect on the landscape of extracting the raw materials to the resource use of the packaging is a complicated exercise that has been applied to only a small part of our output.

Now we have a new externality. Using energy by burning fossil fuel turns out to be causing climatic damage. If the damage is costed and added to the price of fossil fuels as a carbon tax or in some other form, then alternatives to fossil fuel will become more attractive economically.

We can concentrate on energy and materials efficiency with the aim of achieving sustainability. Until now, efficiency has meant primarily labour efficiency, getting the job done with the minimum number of man-hours. As one group of authors write: 'Since the beginning of the Industrial Revolution we have increased our productive capacities by substituting resources for human labour. Yet that substitution has now gone too far, over-using such resources as energy, materials, water, soil and air.'[4] We now understand that labour is a renewable resource.

We can raise awareness of energy efficiency. Most people know how many miles per gallon (mpg) their car does, but not how many kilowatts their refrigerator or computer uses. Things are moving. The EU is now requiring manufacturers of some appliances to state its energy efficiency.

We can use subsidies to shorten the payback time in energy savings. Surveys have found that the average householder is not logical about payback times, expecting a much quicker return than on her savings. She will not pay extra for a more efficient appliance unless it pays for itself in savings within two years.

We can halt or reduce subsidies to fossil fuel-burning activities. The US government still subsidizes the oil, gas and coal industries through depletion allowances and tax breaks. Germany subsidizes the coal industry in order to have a coal industry, and for the otherwise laudable aim of avoiding throwing mining towns on the dole. Greenpeace has produced figures to show that western European countries have spent a billion dollars in the past nine years subsidizing conventional fuels with low royalties for oil extraction, tax breaks and direct subsidies, more than $400 million on nuclear power, and only $149 million on renewables. Britain spent ten times as much on fossil fuel and more than 20 times as much on nuclear power as it did on renewable energy. Even in Denmark, the world leader in wind power, the government spends more money funding oil exploration than it does on renewables. Vast subsidies to agriculture encourage intensive farming and monoculture, both of which damage the environment.

We can distinguish between sustainable and non-sustainable income. For several years recently, Indonesia registered a growth rate of 9 per cent a year. This made it seem like an economic success story to be emulated by other developing countries. However, much of this came from the sale of timber, and the timber value of its forests was reduced by an estimated 40 per cent. This did not include environmental damage. Any business would count this as loss of capital, not income. In what we are taking from the environment, we are all living on capital.

We can ensure that improvements in efficiency are linked to benefits. An architect is paid according to the cost of a building he or she has designed and will not be paid more if it costs less to maintain and to heat. In rented accommodation, the landlord normally buys the equipment for lighting and heating and the tenant pays the running costs. It does not pay the landlord to put lagging in the roof or buy a more efficient refrigerator, since the tenant gets the benefit.

The most innovative social invention designed to increase energy efficiency is 'negawatts', a system by which a utility earns more money by supplying less power. A householder pays for kilowatt-hours of electricity or units of gas. But we don't want kilowatt-hours or units of gas; we want the end product: light and heat, television and cold drinks in the refrigerator. The electricity and the gas are a means of providing these.

The more power the utility provides to give us these things, the more money it makes. But if the utility sold the end product and not the means, then the kilowatts and the units of gas would be a cost, not a profit. It would be in the company's interest to keep the house warm and the refrigerator cold using as little electricity or gas as possible, which means using as little fuel as possible.

Negawatts began in California, an innovator in many areas of environmental action. The state's Public Utilities Commission established a set of rules in 1990 by which a utility that saved energy for its customers could keep some of the profits. A company can make money if it persuades its customers to use more energy-efficient light bulbs or appliances. It is making a profit from 'nega-watts', the electricity it does not sell.

The Pacific Gas and Electric Company, the largest utility in California, planned in the early 1980s to build between 10 and 20 new power stations. It did not build any. Instead, following the change in the rules, the company went in for energy-saving, advising its customers, both domestic and industrial. It has saved more than $300 million a year in energy, of which the company got 15 per cent and the customers the rest.

Southern California Edison Electric subsidizes the manufacture of fluorescent lamps, which consume much less electricity than filament lamps, and it has given a million of them to customers. Many regulatory bodies in America now have some such scheme. British Columbia Hydro subsidizes more efficient electrical motors for Western Canada's mining and pulp paper plants.

The idea has come to Britain although, characteristically, the British company does not use the snappy word 'negawatts' and does not publicize it. Eastern Generation, which used to be Eastern

Electricity, based in Ipswich, has a contract with the City of London to maintain buildings at a specified comfortable temperature, supplying heating or cooling. Eastern Generation decides how much power it has to use and what equipment it installs to achieve this.

The market in energy could be opened up to small producers, even individuals, to encourage efficient production. In parts of Europe and America, utilities have to buy electricity from a supplier if it is cheaper than the electricity they sell. In some places this electricity is subsidized if it is produced by renewable energy. In Germany this has given a boost to wind power. Anyone who chooses to have PV roof cells, or a wind turbine connected to their electricity supply, can have a two-way meter, which records the amount of electricity coming from the grid and also the amount that is being fed back into it. The bill (or the payment from the electricity company) is the difference between the two. The solar-heated house in Richmond has two meters, one to register incoming electricity and other outgoing. It uses the electric company as a storage battery. In the daytime, the house feeds electricity into the grid, which the electric company must pay for. At night, when the solar tiles are not producing any electricity, it buys electricity from the grid.

Everyone has seen or at least heard about the exciting new technologies that can produce energy without burning fossil fuel. But in the near future, the biggest savings in energy will come from boring things like improving efficiency in industry and in buildings. It is cheaper to save energy than to produce it.

Just how much can be done when the incentive is there was seen in the 1970s. Until then, GNP was correlated precisely with energy use. A rise in goods and services provided, in other words, standard of living, meant the same rise in energy used. Then, in

1973, came the jump in oil prices brought in by OPEC. Energy became more expensive, and conserving it meant money saved. In the next 12 years, the GNP in OECD countries rose by 21 per cent but energy use actually fell, by 6 per cent. In the US, energy efficiency rose by 24 per cent, saving $160 billion a year.

This is a pattern. A table of fuel consumption among industrialized countries with roughly the same high standard of living shows that the cheaper the fuel, the less careful people are about saving it, and the higher the per capita consumption. America is the most profligate, Canada and Australia are nearby, the European countries use less and Japan, where fuel prices are highest, uses less still.

One problem in motivating industry to save energy is that energy typically accounts for only 3–4 per cent of manufacturing costs in Europe, and less in America, so there is a tendency to give other things higher priority.

It will come as no surprise to anyone to learn that organizations and industrial plants operate at less than maximum efficiency. It may come as a surprise to hear how *much* less, and how much can be done when people turn their minds to it.

In 1981, a senior engineer at the Dow Chemical Company's Louisiana Division offered incentives to its 2400 employees to come up with ideas to save energy. In each of the next 12 years, changes were implemented. Most meant spending money but these yielded an average return on the investment of 200 per cent. One surprise was that there was no law of diminishing returns. Later savings were as big or bigger than the earlier ones. Once people started thinking about saving energy, they came up with more and more ideas.

We use 29 per cent of our fuel in buildings, for lighting and heating and household appliances. Britain's Building Research Establishment produced a report in December 1995 which listed 20 measures to save fuel all of which could pay back their investment in a short space of time. The IPCC says technologies which have a payback time of only five years can reduce carbon emissions from buildings by 20 per cent by 2010.

Thousands of pages can be filled – thousands of pages *have* been filled – with accounts of how we can save energy with new technologies that are being developed. This is not a book about technology, and besides, the point to make here is that the deciding factor is not technology but the will to seek it out and apply it. Nevertheless, it is worthwhile looking at some of the things that are around that can help us move to a lower-carbon world.

Take buildings. Buildings with solid walls facing the sun absorb heat. New technologies are available: new kinds of window glass that let in and retain heat (the Rocky Mountain Institute is a prime example); new coatings for glass that adjust to the light, exterior fans which ensure than the air does not become stale, allowing more insulation; mirror systems which allow natural light to be reflected down into a room; a pipe that brings in air under the foundations so that it picks up the heat of the earth (even on the coldest days, the earth is warm 10 feet underground).

In Israel if you look across the rooftops, you see solar panels at a 45-degree angle on top of every building. These trap and retain the Sun's heat and heat water that circulates through the building, providing hot water and a degree of central heating. Mass-produced, they could be cheap enough to be put on the rooftops in other countries in the same climate belt.

There are plenty of buildings that show what can be done with existing technology if energy saving is made a prime consideration. The School of Engineering at De Montfort University in Leicester, opened in 1993, is a pink brick structure built around small court-yards that double as outdoor classrooms. The lighting is natural daylight most of the time and ventilation controls temperature. It uses less than 50 per cent of the fuel of an equivalent-size building and cost no more. Architects in St Louis, Missouri, achieved something equally impressive and certainly of wide relevance; a row of old brick and stone houses, leaky and askew with warped walls and windows, were renovated and insulated ingeniously so that heating bills were cut by 90 per cent.

Western governments are willing now to pay to reduce carbon emissions and they are instituting taxes and subsidies. But some studies indicate that the reductions will cost nothing, and will turn out to be no-regrets measures, or, to use the more current term, win–win measures.

* * *

One man whose ideas are likely to contribute to a lower-carbon world is Amory Lovins, the founder and research director of the Rocky Mountain Institute, and an optimistic evangelist for energy efficiency. He is an engineer, environmental campaigner and social philosopher, and one of the inventors of negawatts. Lovins worries about climate change but he says: 'We ought to be purchasing energy efficiency to save money. If we do it right, the environmental benefit comes free.'

Lovins goes much further than most in his assessments of what can be done. He says that with present technology and the newest materials we can build a comfortable, affordable 90 mpg car, ultra-light with ultra-low drag. Given such assertions, he could easily be dismissed as a pie-in-the-sky dreamer. But as a consultant he has the ear of governments and business, and the *Wall Street Journal* once named him as one of the 28 people most likely to change business in the years ahead.

An upright figure with a black bushy moustache, and a graduate of Harvard and Oxford, he goes around the world consulting and lecturing to academic, business and government organizations, throwing out ideas illustrated by slides and charts in a rapid, fluent delivery. He holds up a compact fluorescent light bulb and tells his audience: 'This represents 662 pounds of coal or 62 gallons of oil. That's what will be saved over the bulb's lifetime if you substitute it for a conventional bulb. And the bulb more than pays for itself over its lifetime. This isn't a free lunch. It's a lunch they pay you to eat.'

For Lovins efficiency is much more than an economic question. He wants to empower people and create a greater sense of community and less dependence on remote, inaccessible power centres. As he has written: 'The energy problem should not be how to expand supplies to meet the postulated extrapolated needs of a dynamic economy, but rather how to accomplish social goals elegantly with a minimum of energy and effort, meanwhile taking care to preserve a social fabric that not only tolerates but encourages diverse values and life styles.'[4]

He makes connections. He says that increasing the fuel efficiency of the average American car from 19 mpg to 32 mpg would have replaced the oil the United States imported from Kuwait and Iraq before the Gulf War. 'Did we put our kids in 0.5 mpg tanks and 17-feet-per-gallon aircraft carriers because we failed to put them in 32 mpg cars?' he asks.[6]

Problems are related to one another, and so are solutions. Finding the right way to use energy, he says, is likely to produce a healthier environment and a more liveable community. He and his colleagues at the Rocky Mountain Institute have ideas about energy saving in every area of production and consumption, from computer controls that ensure that electric motors deliver only the power that is needed and no more, to changing a desktop computer screen so that it uses only 10 per cent of the power by using the technology of the laptop, to lighting systems that adjust automatically to the amount of daylight available. They point to instances in which the dramatic savings in energy they envisage have been brought about; the Dow Chemical plant in Louisiana is one of their favourites.

In his latest book,[7] which he co-authored, he takes up the concept of trillion dollar nature (see Chapter 5), and says this 'implies a capitalized book value on the order of half of a quadrillion dollars.' He says industry should regard this as capital, and preserve it as one would any other kind of capital base, instead of using the earth and its resources as wastefully as we do now, and we should aim at spending, not resources, but things that can be renewed, principally labour.

The *Harvard Business Review* publishes his articles, corporations invite him to address them and some give copies of his books to their managers. His fundamental concern is the physical and social environment, but business listens because he tells them how they can make more money.

Saving energy will go a long way towards making the carbon reductions we need. But we will also have to develop new ways of producing energy. The most popular and sought-after form of energy is electricity. Nearly 40 per cent of the world's fossil fuel is burned to drive electric generators. Turbines can be powered by some non-carbon energy source. The electricity carried on the wires between telegraph poles is the same regardless of what drives the turbine that created it.

The principal alternative to fossil fuels to produce electricity that is in use today is nuclear power. This produces no carbon. Industry leaders are pressing its case as a substitute for fossil fuels; nuclear power lobbyists were active at the Buenos Aires conference talking up its benefits. However, it is only profitable with government subsidies, concealed or not, and in any case, post-Chernobyl, the expansion of nuclear power is unacceptable to the public. The amount of nuclear energy in the world is going to shrink as power stations close down and are not replaced. It could make a come-back. It is conceivable that a disaster-proof nuclear power plant can be designed; not accident-proof – there is no such thing – but disaster-proof, one in which a dangerous build-up of radioactivity is physically impossible. Indeed, some nuclear engineers claim that this is true of today's reactors.

The other main fuel for electricity production today is hydro-power. Hydro-electric dams produce no carbon. However, there is little scope for more large-scale hydro projects in developed countries.

Expanding non-fossil fuels means renewables: solar power, bio-mass, wind power, wave power; there are many kinds and each has its applicability. None is price-competitive at present but this is a function of the economic system. With so many subsidies in opera-tion there is no free market in power.

Whether an energy system is economic depends on the cost of the alternatives. Nuclear power was developed in Britain before America because coal and oil cost more in Britain. Renwables are becoming more competitive as taxes on fossil fuels are brought in to pay for the damage to the climate. Joseph Romm, the US Department of Energy official in charge of renewables, says: 'If carbon is taxed, the new technology of renewables becomes unbelievably attractive. With a tax of fifty dollars a ton on carbon, people will be installing windmills as fast as the manufacturers can make them.'[8]

Wind power is the most widely used, a technology that was invented in the Middle East 1000 years ago and spread to Europe, and has now been revived. The old-fashioned windmill has become a wind turbine, using modern materials and linked to an electric generator rather than a grain mill. The sight of wind turbines, with the elongated propellers on spindly poles that have replaced the windmill's sails, is becoming familiar. It is also an undesirable sight in many eyes, and local groups often oppose their installation on aesthetic grounds. They have high visibility because they are going to be situated in wind-swept places: a hilltop or ridge, or a flat prairie. However, wind turbines take up less space than most forms of power generation, no more than the platform on which the turbine stands, and so they can be sited in the middle of farms.

Wind power has grown by more than 20 per cent a year for the last ten years, while oil has grown by less than 2 per cent and coal not at all. The cost of wind-produced electricity fell by 10 per cent a year between 1980 and 1995. The first generation of wind turbines broke down often but they are now a mature technology. Germany is the world leader with more than 2000 megawatts, and Spain is next with about half as much.

Denmark is the biggest user per capita, getting 10 per cent of its electricity from wind power; it plans to increase the amount and to build a new generation of wind turbines offshore. It has a cooperative scheme in which citizens are invited to take part, and now more than 100,000 own shares. It is also a major exporter of wind turbines. The British government expects wind turbines to be a major contributor to its hoped-for reduction in carbon emissions by 2010.

Wind power has potential in the developing countries. India is beginning to exploit it and the government is encouraging the growth of a domestic wind turbine industry. China has just set up its first wind farm with Dutch help.

Biomass, burning wood or other plant material, is classed as a new renewable although it is the oldest fuel in the world. In many parts of the world today, people cook and heat their homes with wood and cow dung, choking on the fumes. Today people are finding more sophisticated ways of using it. European governments are sponsoring schemes to encourage farmers to plant fast-growing trees to burn in power plants, and replace the trees. This means taking as much carbon out of the air in the growing trees as the burning puts in. The EU is currently paying farmers to set aside land and do nothing with it; it would make more sense to pay them to grow fuel on the land.

Perhaps the most promising form of electric power is the photovoltaic cells or PVs, that line the roof of that house in Richmond. Tiny PVs are found in wristwatches and pocket calculators and most of us are familiar with these. The PV does not drive a turbine. It is the simplest form of electricity generation, with no heat and no moving parts, a silicon-coated cell that transforms sunlight into an electric current. Panels composed of PVs are useful in places far from an electric grid such as oil rigs, and can supply electricity in rural villages in the developing world.

The newest idea is to use them as cladding on roofs and external walls, which reduces the cost since they serve a double function. They keep the lights burning in the main building of the University of Northumbria, and a housing estate in Essen, and in the YKK office building in Tokyo. They are not competitive with grid electricity where it is available, but as production grows by 20 per cent a year the price is coming down, and will come down further with economies of scale. The Japanese government plans to have 100,000 PV roofs within five years. Demand may soon be so great that manufacturers will have to find a new source of silicon; at present they use scrap from computer manufacturers.

Photovoltaic cells and wind power could be the answer to the developing world's demand for electricity. Other kinds of renewable energy are more place-specific. Norway with its long North Sea coastline has developed wave power machines that contribute to the electricity grid.

The big fuel companies are getting the message. Shell is investing $500 million in renewable energy, including biomass and solar power, and it is manufacturing PVs. Shell's former managing director, the group chairman, Cor Herkstroter, dismayed his former GCC allies by announcing that the group favoured global reductions of carbon by 5 per cent, and said Shell is disposing of its coal assets. (These generate less than 1 per cent of its earnings so this is not a major move.) British Petroleum has set up PV systems all over the world and sells one designed for individual homes, which it markets as 'the sun in a box'. Solar power is no longer an environmental crusade. It is a business.

Shell and British Petroleum are still exploring for oil, and so are the other power companies. To some extent these new departures are simply a matter of keeping options open. The companies also want to look environment-friendly. One hopes that some of them also want to *be* environment-friendly, and to exercise some social responsibility. Corporation executives also have grandchildren.

Corporations are no more monoliths than governments. The setting-up of renewable energy sections means that they now have executives with a vested interest in changing direction and they are likely to be pressing for this. Mac Moore, the chief executive of BP Solar, says: 'My feeling is that we're at the point in time where the personal computer was in the late 1970s. If things go well, there's going to be a revolutionary change in the way we obtain power.' Ford's director of environmental vehicles, John Wallace, says: 'The world is moving from carbon-based to hydrogen-based fuel.'

It seems likely that we are moving, if slowly, out of the fossil fuel age, 100 years old in the case of oil, 300 years in the case of coal.[9] For one thing, whereas there are enough known reserves of oil to last for a century at least, oil industry experts say supply will peak around the middle of the century and after that the price will rise.

Hydrogen may well be the principal source of power in the post-fossil fuel age. Burning hydrogen releases gas under pressure that can be used for any purpose, and it produces no carbon and few pollutants. Scenarios have been constructed in which hydrogen is separated out from the other gases with which it usually combines in huge plants using solar power, and then used as a fuel.

Fuel cells using hydrogen are a closer prospect. In a fuel cell, the hydrogen atoms are ionized, producing electricity, and then combined with oxygen. The only waste product is water. Some engineers also envisage them being used as a small power plants, so that each building would have its own, but they are designed principally for use in cars.

* * *

Much of the attention of the environmentalist movement is focused on cars. To the puritans in the environmental movement, the car is a symbol of selfish greed, its high performance engine a sign of boastful machismo, its sleek, gleaming shape a manifestation of vanity, its exhaust an assault on the population. For these people, taxing cars off our roads is not an unfortunate necessity but a moral duty.

Motor vehicles contribute a quarter of the carbon we put into the atmosphere. There are some 560 million on the world's roads. It is easy to see why so much attention is focused on the situation if you stand on a main road leading into any big city around eight o'clock in the morning and watch the thousands of cars streaming in, each carrying one person. The amount of metal, oil and space taken up and air polluted to transport each individual presents a staggering view of the wastefulness of our society.

Another is the news-stands in a big American city on Sunday evening, the stacks of unsold newspapers, each 250-plus pages, produced the day before, with a shelf-life measured in hours, now garbage waiting to be picked up. How long before this resource-wasteful method of distributing information is superseded?)

The US is ahead of the rest of the world in car ownership, with one car to 1.6 people, although Europe is catching up. Americans have more cars not only because petrol is cheap in the US but also because land is less expensive. American communities are much more spread out than European ones and further apart from one another. (In a motel in Arizona once, I asked where the nearest bank was and was told, 'Down the road on the left'. 'How far?' I asked. 'Forty-five miles.') In a typical American suburb or small town each house is on its own plot of land with space on all four sides. To walk to the end of the street to reach the shops or anywhere else is likely to be a long walk. Local bus services are few. For many people, to go anywhere except to their next-door neighbour means a car journey. The home with two bedrooms and three cars is not only commonplace but functional. Even Homer and Marge Simpson are a two-car family.

It is recognized now that getting people to travel on public transport rather than in their own cars is a public good, and a contribution to curbing climate change. Freight transport by road uses eight to ten times more energy than by rail. Governments are acting to discourage driving and improve public transport, but most could do more. Naturally this is being resisted by the car and petroleum industries.

Trends in our society make for more car ownership. Super-markets are forcing small shops out of business, so that people now do their shopping in bulk and by car. Entertainment also is being concentrated. Multiplex cinemas mean local cinemas closing down. People in rural areas have to use their cars more so rural transport shrinks and they have to use their cars even more.

Changes have to be made from the ground up, literally. Our cities and towns have adapted to the car; now they can reverse the process. Curitiba, a city of 1.5 million people in southern Brazil, is held up as an example of what can be done. Because it has tripled its population in 25 years, town planners and architects could design its expansion. They laid out broad avenues designed to provide access between residential and business areas, bus lanes and articulated buses. They invented a new kind of boarding system in which passengers buy their tickets on a boarding pod and enter through several doors, as in a tube station, which speeds throughput. There are express and local buses and a low fare. Curitiba has the highest car ownership of any city in Brazil and the lowest number of cars on the road.

The Netherlands cannot rebuild its cities, but it has a national environmental plan designed to discourage cars. It is trying to prevent greater separation of work, shopping and living areas, improve public transport and encourage cycling. One small example: employees used to get a small supplement to their salaries if they had to travel a distance to work, to cover the cost of transport. Now they get a supplement if they live close to their work. Singapore will not allow cars with only person in the city. In Manchester, the establishment of an integrated tram, bus and train transport system has reduced car journeys by 2.7 million a year.

Most countries in Europe tax cars according to their engine size. The driver who emits the most carbon pays the most tax. Road taxes and petrol taxes are being increased.

However, no tax is going to get cars off the roads. People like having their own personal transport. In the early 1970s the price of petrol trebled in the space of three years. Sales took only a slight dip and then continued rising. The rising price of petrol in Britain today has made no difference to the number of cars on the roads, and this is not simply a perverse obsession with the car, as some would claim. For a car-owner, it makes economic sense to drive. It is usually cheaper than going by rail. The biggest cost by far of a car is the purchase price. Taking into account the purchase price, depreciation, insurance and road tax, the petrol is only about a sixth of the cost of driving each extra mile.

Since a lot of people are going to want to drive cars, an answer to carbon emissions is to design a different kind of car. The biggest boost for this effort came from the California legislature, which has ruled that 10 per cent of cars sold in the state in 2003 must emit no carbon.

The favoured fuel to replace petrol is ethanol, produced from plants, which emits hardly any carbon. In Brazil today, most cars run on ethanol mixed with petrol. Brazilian cities have traffic jams but little pollution from cars. The ethanol is produced from sugar cane, and requires government subsidies to make it viable. But biotechnologists say ethanol can now be produced from any plant, thanks to catalysts created by genetic manipulation, and this is price-competitive with petrol. The feed material could be crops grown for the purpose or even farm waste, which is cost-free. The US Federal Aviation Authority recently licensed a new aircraft fuel that is 87 per cent ethanol, for use in light propeller-driven planes.

This is a change in technology that would create large social and political changes. The fuel would come from the world's farms, not from a few small countries situated on top of oilfields. As the authors of an article on the subject that was praised by President Clinton wrote: 'If the hundreds of billions of dollars that now flow into a few coffers in a few nations were to flow instead to the millions of people who till the world's fields, most countries would see substantial national security, economic and environmental benefits.'[10]

Using ethanol means adapting the internal combustion engine, and this can be done inexpensively. But some people think the car powered by the internal combustion engine will pass into history. The chairman of General Motors, John Smith, surprised his audience at the 1998 Detroit Auto Show when he told them. 'No car company will be able to thrive in the 21st century if it relies solely on internal combustion engines.'

All major car manufacturers are working on a substitute. The US government is financing a cooperative effort by the big three manufacturers.

One candidate to replace it, at least for some purposes, is the electric car. The magazine *Scientific American* wrote: 'The electric automobile . . . has the great advantage of being silent, free from odour, simple in construction, capable of ready control, and having a considerable range of speed.' That was in 1896. Three years later in France, an electric car, the *Jamais Contente,* broke the world speed record with a speed of 105 kilometres an hour.

In the competition with the petrol-driven car the electric car lost, but now it is on the road again, with the old advantages plus a much more efficient battery. General Motors, Honda, Peugeot and Renault have all produced electric cars, and France, Germany, Switzerland, Austria and Denmark all give tax credits as encouragement to purchase them. However, there are only a few thousand on the roads, and they are expensive. The electric car would change the way people use their cars. It can drive only 100 miles or so before the battery has to be recharged. They could be used for inner-city travel, particularly if petrol-driven cars are banned. In France and Switzerland, car-makers have plans to change the pattern of car ownership and use. People will be able to rent an electric car to drive a short distance, as they would take a cab, and there will be re-charging stations dotted around cities as there are now petrol stations.

Hybrid cars with both petrol and battery-powered engines are being road-tested in California. Toyota is ahead of others with the Prius, a hybrid car that emits little carbon and does 85 mpg. A taxi powered by an electric fuel cell has received a licence to ply for hire in London, and is indistinguishable from other London taxis. Since a fuel cell car is also a mobile electric power plant, a fuel cell car could be plugged into the grid and could deliver electricity to it when it is not being driven, for which the driver could be paid.

As well as saving carbon, we can sequester it. Reforestation soaks up carbon and in the present market in carbon reduction it is the cheapest way to do it. Planting forests in Latin America could be matched in North America by planting prairie grass, which grows down ten feet. Farmers can practise no-till or low-till farming. The soil is not turned over but is refreshed by planting crops of legumes between the cash crops, which soaks up carbon. In some Midwestern states the authorities are trying to encourage this. They have some success with family farms, where the owner expects to leave the farm to his children, less with the large estates owned by agribusinesses. There are also engineered ways of sequestering carbon, such as solidifying it and burying it or funnelling carbon from a power plant into the sea.

Measures can be taken to restrict methane emissions. Methane from landfill sites can be stored, and much of the biological waste that now produces methane can be recycled. Leakage from mining and petrochemicals could be cut by a third. Sir John Houghton has calculated that this could cut total greenhouse gas emissions by 5 per cent.

All this can be done without any new inventions. Yet there will be new inventions, as there always are when the demand is there. Work going on now suggests several innovations that might come out of the laboratories in the next few years: a dye that can be spread on to ordinary glass to turn it into a PV; super-hard lightweight materials created at the molecular level by nanotechnology; microbes that can eat carbon as others now eat iron and chlorine. The far future holds out yet more possibilities.

We do not know now which ones of these technologies will be most important in the future. The crucial question is not technological. It is how hard we try, how hard management tries, what priority government gives it, and what consumers want.

Government can do much with taxes and subsidies. Several governments are stepping up the promotion of research in these areas, but they are still spending only a fraction of what they spend on defence-related research, in aviation and nuclear energy, for instance. Climate change is also a threat to national security.

Considering this explosion of new technology and moves in several directions, we should refer back to what is happening in China. The most significant thing is not that China, the largest developing country, reduced its carbon emissions, nor even that it did so while still maintaining economic growth. What is most significant is that it did so *while it was trying to do something else.* China was trying to save energy, cut pollution and save money. Reducing greenhouse gas emissions was a by-product.

This does not mean that we can reduce our carbon emissions without making an effort. It means that when we do so, we may also be doing all those other things as well. Reducing greenhouse gases may turn out to be only a part of a big shift in the way we use energy and in our sources of energy, a shift that will change all our lives. It also means that in the long and even the medium term, the cost of curbing climate change may be negative, that the benefits stemming from the measures we take may outweigh the price. This would reduce the cost-benefit calculations of avoiding climate change to irrelevance.

If the world envisaged in all these changes seems difficult to imagine, this is only because we tend to forget how quickly the exotic becomes familiar. We live in a time of rapid change. Look, for instance, at the changes people have absorbed in the last 50 years, a period well within a normal life span and within the memory of many people who will be reading this.

Fifty years ago, there was no jet travel, nuclear power, space satellites, colour television, home computers, cassette players or videos. There were no credit cards, ATM machines, photocopiers, plastic shopping bags or frozen food, and much of what appears in print and in the media today would have earned its perpetrators a term of penal servitude.

If, 50 years from now, the view of a city from the air is rooftops of photovoltaic cells, if a petrol-powered car is as rare on the roads as a horse and cart is today and a battery charging station is found in every high street, if plastic is grown on farms and disposed of by microbes, if fluorescent bulbs are the only ones you see in homes, if small towns have their own power source supplied by solar energy, most power stations use hydrogen as a fuel, and the new ones under construction use a source of energy that today is only a scientist's wild idea, then these changes will be no more dramatic than those that have taken place in the last 50 years, and almost certainly less dramatic than other unrelated changes that will have taken place over the same period.

CHAPTER **8**

NEAR FUTURE,
FAR FUTURE

I shall be content with the possibility of unlimited progress – or progress subject to no limits that we can or need envisage – towards goals which can be defined only as we advance towards them, and the validity of which can be verified only in a process of obtaining them – EH Carr[1]

A CRUISE LINER is at sea. The charts show that a few days' sailing ahead of them is a minefield. The Captain has his problems, as captains do. The engine-room crew are one man short, there's been a complaint about the restaurant service, and a rainstorm heading their way might force the cancellation of the deck tennis tournament. On the other hand, he has reason to be optimistic. He and his senior officers have been promised a pay bonus if a number of the passengers are so pleased that they will book a cruise with this line again, and several have said they might.

The first mate is at his elbow. 'The minefield, sir. We're still on course for it. What are we going to do?'

The Captain ponders this. He has never had to think about mines before. This was not included in the job description. 'Hmmm, yes. It's a problem. Get an officer assigned to it. Have him draw up some options. And be ready to re-schedule the deck tennis tournament. Now about the restaurant service. It's important for all of us that everything goes well. . .'

The priority that governments give to threats to the planetary environment is still disproportionate to their seriousness. This is partly due to the novelty of the threats. They are very different to the problems with which governments are accustomed to deal.

They require action which a government cannot take on its own, and getting the cooperation of others always means compromising and falling in with other people's ways of doing things. The consequences of action or inaction will be in the future, in many cases in the far future, which means thinking outside the traditional terms of politics. As the sociologist David Goldblatt writes: 'Global environmental problems have stretched the normative time-horizon of political discourse, and introduced the notion of inter-generational justice and sustainability into our political-moral vocabulary.'[2]

The threats can be met. The ship can change course. It requires ingenuity, new ways of doing things, some adaptation in ways of living. It does not require great sacrifice, of the kind that governments urge on their populations or force on them during a war. It means giving up some of the old ways, something that most people, governments included, are usually reluctant to do.

So governments continue to tell people to go on getting rich in the same way and continue to expand their economies using the same criteria, with an occasional brief detour in favour of the environment. They are qualifying economic growth instead of re-defining it. They are ignoring the fact that the present process is not sustainable, that in our relations with the material world we are living on capital rather than income, that we are damaging the environment on which we depend, not only by changing the climate but in other ways as well.

Yet new ideas are spreading, and there are signs of change. We have responded successfully to local environmental degradation. In most Western cities the air is cleaner than it was and in most Western rivers the water is more pure. New ideas about the economy and about our interaction with the planetary environment are spreading, through industry and through governments. There is reason to hope that the steamroller of economic growth will be given a steering wheel.

On climate change, one can see several scenarios. The Kyoto process may succeed. Industry will reconcile itself to reducing emissions of greenhouse gases and will see that the strain of having to change is matched by benefits. There will be some losers – coal miners will lose their jobs and oil share prices will fall – but they will be helped where possible, and a dwindling minority will not be able to block progress. In this scenario, the US Senate ratifies the treaty and the US, as well as buying emission quotas, makes enough reductions on its own to show that it is serious. Several EU countries exceed their reduction targets. At the next negotiating stage, after 2010, all nations agree to reduce emissions. Funds are made available through the GEF, to enable developing countries to reduce emissions and to bribe them to do so. Developing nations improve efficiency and turn to newer methods of power generation as they enlarge their industries.

The weather continues to become warmer and there are more climatic disasters, but warming eventually halts. By now a treaty regime is in place, functioning. This is the contractual route.

There is another scenario. The US Senate refuses to ratify the Kyoto Protocol and developing countries denounce the whole process. But the new ideas about using less energy spread through industry. Saving energy is seen to make business sense. With a push from public opinion, new technologies of power generation and transport are taken up. British and American industry are no longer content to see Denmark as the leading exporter of wind turbines and Germany of PVs, and they develop their own manufacturing base and create domestic markets.

Poorer countries see new ways to develop, taking their lead from China and from technical developments in the West. Coal becomes yesterday's fuel. When the Kyoto Protocol parties next meet, one nation after another promises to reduce its greenhouse gas emissions, which in most cases are declining anyway. Developing countries are under pressure to follow suit and see advantages in doing so. This is one kind of multi-unilateral route.

Another scenario is a continuing rise in temperatures with climatic disasters and no agreement. Some countries, perhaps the wealthiest Western countries, reduce their emissions but not enough and all suffer the effects of global warming. These countries subsidize their agricultural sector to allow it to adjust to new conditions, compete for overseas supplies of food and raw materials for themselves, and build sea walls around the areas most vulnerable to flooding. Some tropical and semi-tropical countries, being too poor to take such measures, experience horrendous droughts and floods, millions starve to death, and some populated islands have to be abandoned. There is turbulence and a flow of refugees. It is a more unhappy, more dangerous and more conflict-prone world.

In the long-run, international action on climate change is best guaranteed if it is contractual, that is, enshrined in a binding agreement. The agreement will have to include sanctions against rogue states that refuse to abide by its terms, since otherwise, there would be areas of the world in which anyone could go and do whatever they liked to the atmosphere. It may have to intrude further into sovereign territory. If reduction of carbon emissions proved inadequate it might give to some supra-national body the power to impose the rules in countries where the national authority is unable to do so. This would shade towards eco-hegemony.

Although carbon dioxide is often called a pollutant, it is not. There is nothing inherently unhealthy in an atmosphere that contains twice as much carbon dioxide as the present one and a global climate that is one or two degrees warmer. If that had been the atmosphere and the climate during the last 10,000 years, civilization would still have developed. But it would have developed in different ways. Different crops would have been planted, communities would have been established in different places. We have adapted to the present climate instead of another.

We can adapt to some change. Climate change before we have time to adapt will produce hardship and suffering. What is at issue is how much damage will be inflicted. With the great difficulty we have in reaching collective decisions, things may deteriorate a long way producing a great deal of hardship, perhaps unprecedented hardship, before the process of change is halted or slowed down sufficiently. Or we may take effective action sooner.

Climate change is only the most urgent of the environmental challenges that face us. Others may in the long run prove as important. Most are susceptible to the same kind of approach. Most international action can be contractual, multi-lateral or, in most cases, eco-hegenomic.

Biodiversity already has a treaty but it is a weak one. There are regular meetings of the parties, and they may decide to strengthen it, which will mean the industrial countries ceding more ground to the poorer countries, within whose borders most of the effort to preserve biodiversity must be made. But again, it is also possible that governments and multinational corporations, perhaps under some consumer pressure, may act themselves, and take a series of unilateral measures. Undoubtedly the situation will get worse, we will suffer more loss of species at a rate unprecedented for the last 65,000 years, and we and future generations will be poorer for it.

Other situations will arise which also can best be managed, or can only be managed, on a planet-wide basis. They will arise because of the impact we make on the biosphere in our efforts to achieve a more comfortable life.

The use of chemical fertilizers, particularly nitrogen, to increase the productivity of the soil has long been giving concern to ecologists. Its effects are now spreading far beyond the areas in which it is used, through the food chain and into the oceans. The UNEP report *Global Environment Outlook 2000* says: 'Consensus among researchers is growing that the scale of disruption to the nitrogen cycle may have global implications comparable to those caused by disruption of the carbon cycle.'[3]

Antarctica may be an issue at some time in the future. It was not difficult to reach an agreement to protect Antarctica as a global common because nothing was to be gained by exploiting it. There is mineral wealth there, but it cannot be extracted profitably. But mining techniques change and will change more, perhaps with the introduction of remote-controlled robot miners, or genetically engineered micro-organisms that extract minerals. At that point there will have to be a stronger treaty to prevent exploitation of the continent or an international consensus on managing it.

The oceans are a global commons and the source of much of the food that humankind eats. They are being over-fished. Sixty per cent of the world's ocean fisheries are being fished at or near the limit of sustainability, and international agreements to prevent over-fishing are proving inadequate.

The most urgent material problem is the shortage of fresh water, which affects everyone. Warm summers in England mean a ban on sprinklers in gardens. Many western American states live permanently on the edge of a water shortage and their populations are increasing rapidly. It is a political problem. Syria controls Israel's source of fresh water, the Jordan River flowing into the Dead Sea, and a hostile Turkey controls Syria's in the Tigris River. Egypt has threatened to go to war if Sudan dams the Nile.

Worldwide, the reduction of top soil threatens food supply. So far the human race has beaten the gloomy Malthusian prediction by technology, keeping ahead of expanding population by increasing food productivity. Although there are more hungry people in the world than ever before, this is because there are more people. Per capita food consumption has increased in the past half-century, but the amount of top soil may prove to be a limiting factor.

It is very likely that we will face new environmental challenges that we do not envisage now. We are putting new chemicals into the atmosphere and the ground all the time and employing new technologies, and we cannot know all their effects as they interact. CFCs destroying the ozone layer came as a surprise. Greenhouse gases changing the climate came as a surprise. We can expect more surprises.

Principles established in the process of negotiating the Kyoto Protocol can be adapted to other agreements on the global environment and they are likely to be. As in the climate change agreements, rich and poor countries will be given different targets or tasks and different responsibilities. Environment protection or repair will be globalized, as it is in joint implementation and the Clean Development Mechanism; the environmental protection measures that a government takes will not be limited to its own territory.

An agreement will be flexible, like the Framework Convention on Climate Change and the Kyoto Protocol. Like these, they will be agreements in principle on aims, with a framework into which figures are slotted. Any firm targets will be for limited periods only, so that they can be extended or adapted later to changed circumstances, findings or perspectives. As time goes by and we learn more, and are able to accomplish more, an environmental threat may become more urgent or less urgent. Our ways of living and the machines by which we live change, and this may create new problems or it may solve problems. What is a damaging situation today may not be a problem a century or two centuries from now.

* * *

National governments act selfishly. That is what they are set up to do, to improve the well-being of their people. However, these days they do not like to be seen to be acting selfishly. People do not want to be told that their leaders have enriched them at the expense of others. No one today would say admiringly of a national leader, as Shakespeare's Marc Antony says of Julius Caesar, 'He hath brought many captives home to Rome whose ransoms did the general coffers fill'.

None the less governments, and particularly democratic governments that are answerable to the voters, believe that what their people really want is to maintain and improve their standard of living, and they believe their people will judge them according to whether this has been achieved. This is why they frequently ignore opinion polls that show that voters want their governments to contribute to global well-being and to act generously.

Classical political realism pictures nations as discreet entities each acting only in its own national interest, narrowly defined. Planetary management is compatible with this picture. The realist view allows for a nation joining a system that works for the general good in order to protect its own interests – a defence or trade alliance, for instance. But focusing on the welfare of the entire planet, and on the legacy we will leave to future generations, challenges the limits of classical realism. Several other factors operating in the world also challenge the classical realist view, and the people who deal with international issues have to think beyond traditional categories.

Some writers foresee the end of the nation-state, but this is at the least premature. The nation-state is still going to be the most important actor in the process of managing the planet for some time to come. It is the principal entity able to make laws and enforce rules. But nation-states are not the only actors, and their situation and role is changing.

The present system of states is sometimes called the Westphalian system, after the 1648 Treaty of Westphalia. In this treaty, which ended the religious wars that were devastating central Europe, it was agreed that a ruler exercises sole sovereignty in his or her own territory and others have no right to interfere. Over the years this convention became the formal basis of relations between nations. It survived the transition from the age of princes to the age of democracy. When Britain and France declared war on Germany in 1939 they condemned the wickedness of the Nazi government, but they did not suggest that this was the reason they had gone to war. What the Nazi government did within its own borders was considered to be an internal matter.

Now this system has been eroded. The rules are no longer respected universally. The erosion is due partly to technical developments. International air travel, radio communication, postal services, maritime safety, nuclear power and many other activities all have to be regulated. Everyone must follow the same rules if these systems are to function. International regimes that regulate are not a novelty.

European nations have handed over some of their autonomy to the EU. National governments submit to the rulings of the World Trade Organization (WTO), which tells government what subsidies they may give to their industries and what restrictions they may place on imports. The International Monetary Fund and the World Bank impose conditions on loans that effectively dictate a government's economic policy.

Nation-states as the sole repositories of authority are also challenged from within, as substate groups, ethnic and religious, raise their profile. Some national governments are weak and unable to exert authority over all their territory. These are not only small ex-colonial countries with no tradition of state power; Russia cannot collect taxes from some of its industries, let alone dictate how they may burn fuel.

Multilateral forces have been sent into many countries under the UN or the NATO banner. In 1991 the UN General Assembly broke with the Westphalian principles explicitly when it asserted the right of humanitarian intervention in certain circumstances with or without the consent of the national government. International law has been extended to override national law, so that a war criminal can be tried by an international tribunal, and a person may be tried in one country for certain crimes committed in another.

Other actors are playing bigger parts. Multinational corporations have more economic power than many governments. Terrorist and paramilitary groups, some transnational, shape events. Non-governmental organizations are increasingly influential. Some governments hand over parts of their foreign aid programmes to NGOs such as

Oxfam and Save the Children. The director of the UN Centre for Human Rights, Ibrahim Fall, complained in 1993 that the UN Centre has less money and fewer resources than Amnesty International.

National borders are permeable. More and more international activity is not inter-governmental. Ideas, popular culture and money flow around the world, facilitated by electronic media, whether television or the internet, with little regard for the wishes of governments. Ultimately, a nation-state depends on the loyalty of its citizens and their willingness to identify themselves with it. People in the Western world are less nationalistic, more individualistic, more ready to identify with a lifestyle as well as a nation.

The climate change issue, as it develops and as we deal with it, will weaken the authority of the nation-state further. An agreement means that national governments will have to submit to the rule of an international regime. People will relate to a situation larger than their own nation, weakening the moral authority of national governments. Other global environmental agreements will have the same effect.

Quasi-political movements are now global. The demonstrations against the WTO at the time of its meeting in Seattle in December 1999 were organized over the internet and took place in a dozen cities around the world simultaneously. This is not necessarily democratic. The organizers of the demonstrations were no more elected than multinational corporations, nor were they any more answerable. (Fundamentalist religions are also global, and also use the internet, but are no more democratic for it.) But it is multi-polar. It shows that many groups now have the power to influence events.

Consumers also have power. It was consumer pressure that first forced the manufacturers of aerosols to stop using the ozone-damaging CFCs. Corporations fall over themselves to show their green credentials. Consumer pressure can be as powerful as legislation in determining what business and industry do to the planet.

The Stewardship Councils that have been established over the oceans and the forests are good examples of cooperation on the environment between different actors. Both join together environmental organizations and business. The Marine Stewardship Council, set up in 1996 between the World Wide Fund For Nature and Unilever, supports environmentally friendly fishing practices. It certifies fish products as coming from fisheries that meet these standards and encourages retailers and consumers to choose them. The Forest Stewardship Council has also introduced a labelling scheme to mark out timber products that have come from sustainably maintained forests and major retailers have agreed to buy only these products. Neither stewardship council has any governmental authority. However, they would be strengthened by governmental support.

Most advances in technological ability can be used to benefit the few or the many. Which it is depends on politics, on who has power, and this does not mean only governmental power. Genetic manipulation of organisms has important potentialities; some multinational corporations use it to extend their control over food production at the expense of farmers, particularly in poor countries, and criticism of this is confused with criticism of the process. In fact, genetic engineering of food crops may be one of the less important uses of our new abilities to manipulate genes, much less important than its application to animals and, one day, to humans.

Environmental issues are entwined with economic issues as well as technology. Developing countries will be more willing to participate in global environmental efforts, and communities within these countries more able to do so, if they are less hard-pressed by poverty. Changing a global economic systems that favours the rich countries makes it easier to take action on the environment. Relaxing developing world debt further and changing the rules on commodity prices could also be beneficial. So would a reduction in corruption and nepotism in many developing world governments, so that most people benefit from improvements in the economy and action on the environment is better implemented.

People's material well-being depends on politics and social structures more than any other factor. In 1950 South Korea and Ghana had the same GNP. Today, Korea has the GNP of a Western nation. Brazil has twice the GNP of Sri Lanka, but the distribution of wealth is very unequal, so a Sri Lankan baby has a better chance of surviving infancy and of going to school.

Demands are rising, and if resources shrink and competition for them becomes fiercer, it will be a world of greater deprivation, and therefore a more dangerous one. The powerful will use their power to ensure that they do not lose out and their people continue to get the things they are used to, whatever the cost to others.

Environmentalists like to quote a saying from Pogo, Walt Kelly's comic strip about a group of animals who live in the Louisiana swamps. 'We have met the enemy', Pogo says, 'and he is us.' (This parodies a declaration by an American naval hero of the War of 1812, Commander William Perry, known to American schoolboys: 'We have met the enemy and he is ours.') There is another saying by Pogo that is also worth recalling as we contemplate the prospect of a world of depleted resources. Pogo at one point faces the prospect of being stranded on a desert island with another one of the animals, a tiger, and he says fearfully: 'We'll starve! And when you starve with a tiger, the tiger starves last.'

An agreement on climate change will tend to reduce the gap between rich and poor. The Kyoto Protocol has taken a small step in this direction by imposing obligations on the wealthy countries which are not imposed on the others. Poorer countries have leverage; the wealthy, powerful countries have to buy their cooperation.

Further agreements are likely to have the effect of a graduated income tax, imposing greater burdens on the wealthy and therefore having an equalizing tendency. They will mean the transfer of resources in the form of money or technology from the wealthy to the developing countries to help them develop in ways that are less environmentally damaging. We should be ready to accept this. It will be a community tax, which will be paying for services to the world. This transfer will doubtless provoke opposition among some who will decry it as give-away. However, it can be seen, and sold to the public, as pure self-interest, a counterpart to the funds given now to Russia to enable it to safeguard its nuclear weapons material, which no one disputes is money well spent.

If, following agreement on repairing the ozone layer, governments can agree on managing the climate, they will be building a system of rules and norms and conventions which will provide guidance in future situations in which our impact on the global environment is an issue. This might take its place alongside the present nation-state system or whatever complex of groups with overlapping powers replaces it. As our understanding of our interdependence grows, it would both reflect and enhance the sense of a world community.

What is a community? It is not a happy family or a group of people who never quarrel. It is a collection of people who live in the same neighbourhood. They are not all friends, but they interact continually. They have concerns in common, such as garbage collection and the condition of the roads and local parks. The value of their properties tends to rise or fall together. There are certain activities which damage the community and which all members agree are to be avoided. For the good of all, there are conventions that are followed.

Environmental arrangements, about what we collectively do to the planet, will become more important as time goes on. The nation-state system may dissolve or change. Our impact on the planetary environment will continue, and will need to be managed.

Nations, corporations and even individuals submitting themselves to the rules of an international regime will not be world government. It will not even be a step towards it. It will be governance in a particular area, an extension of the kind of governance we have now in areas which intrude less in our daily lives, such as the use of radio wavelengths and the transport of nuclear material. Like any governance it can be wise or unwise, effective or clumsy. Like any governance also, its effectiveness will depend, not primarily on strict enforcement of the rules, but on a common appreciation of the situation that makes them necessary, and an acceptance of common norms and conventions that support this.

* * *

The title of this book suggests, and is intended to suggest, that the new kind of politics that is required and that is coming into being will extend into the far future, not only well into this new century, but also into the millennium that has just begun.

During the 21st century, we will become still more aware of environmental limitations on our activities. The world may experience economic breakdown and climatic catastrophes because we have not adjusted to these limitations. In the long run we will become more adept at overcoming them. Beyond that, the indications are that our power to affect the biosphere will continue to grow and the problems of managing that power along with it.

The changes that will take place over the next thousand years cannot be imagined, let alone predicted. They will be profound and far-reaching. The model for the rate of change is not the last thousand years but the last three centuries, which includes the Industrial Revolution.

Beyond the near future we can see only dimly, and further than that hardly at all. We cannot predict things of which we cannot conceive. An imaginative person in the middle of the 18th century, when the use of machine power began, might have guessed that people would one day fly through the air, even though they could not say how. They could not have predicted radio or nuclear power. New things will come about that we cannot imagine, but we can look ahead to some developments that have their genesis today.

More and more of the planet will be managed. We will need more of the planet to produce food and other things we need. As we make more impact, we will also have to manage parts of the wilderness, if only to protect them.

People will learn to recycle and reconstitute all materials. No matter is ever destroyed. (This is not literally true. Some radioactivity is the transformation of matter into energy. But the amounts of matter are infinitesimal.) All matter, including organic matter, when it is used up, burned, chopped into pieces, killed or eaten, is simply converted into other forms. In theory, it could be reconstituted in its original form, even if, in the case of an organism, life is not restored. In the centuries ahead we will learn how to reconstitute all matter into the form we want, so that there will be no material shortages, not even of water (which can be desalinated, a process that is too expensive to be practical in most of the world today).

The means of doing this may be genetically engineered micro-organisms, an advance on the ones that can now eat oil slicks.

We will probably be able to reconstitute all living matter, perhaps so skilfully that there will be no shortage of food or of topsoil to grow it in. Just as our forefathers cross-bred seeds and transplanted them across oceans, so our descendants may manipulate and transplant genes and DNA molecules to create new plants and new biological processes.

We will change human beings. As our ability to alter the human organism increases, so more possibilities will open up. Already we are interfering in the natural process of childbirth, with *in vitro* fertilization and delayed menopause. Babies may be produced outside the womb, sparing those women who opt for this the pains and discomforts of childbirth.

Scientists hope to find a way to intervene at the foetal stage to prevent certain diseases, and they will no doubt succeed. But in medicine, there is no clear dividing line between being proactive and reactive, between preventing disease and enhancing health.

Who could argue against producing babies immune from certain diseases? Doctors want to prevent mental retardation. How about intervening to produce a more intelligent person? Who wants a child of only average intelligence? They will want to prevent restricted growth. But most people will want an offspring taller than average, which gives advantages in life. We have the prospect of designer babies.

Perhaps the human brain will be linked directly to computers. Perhaps consciousness will be extended into new forms. Human life may take forms we cannot imagine today.

We will have the power to change the planet directly. Again, reactive action can lead to proactive action. We are acting now to prevent or repair damage to the global environment. We will be able also to improve on the global environment. We could eliminate darkness in a part of the globe by putting large mirrors in a geostationary orbit to reflect the sun when it is over the horizon. That is feasible now. Once the climate is stabilized, and the process of warming is halted, we will one day be able to improve on it. This would have consequences for agriculture, apart from anything else. Population growth may require dramatic measures. We may well decide not to do any of this to our planet. But we will have the option. The process of decision will require new kinds of international politics.

People will explore space. They will probably colonize planets and asteroids, if only to exploit them for their resources. A group of scientists at the National Aeronautics and Space Administration's (NASA) Ames Research Center in Sunnyvale, California have worked out how to 'terraform' Mars, converting its atmosphere into an earth-like one. Satellite mirrors would focus more sunlight on the planet, black soot scattered on the poles would absorb more sunlight causing the ice to melt, and later genetically engineered plants would create an oxygen atmosphere. This sounds quite exciting until they say that it would take 10,000 years. It seems likely that between now and then, people will think of quicker ways to do it.

Mankind will eventually intervene in its own evolution. We can improve on the human species, not, like the process of natural selection, in a blind quest for continuing survival, but in a purposeful way, to reduce the elements within us that make us stupid, short-sighted, selfish and cruel, and expand those that are more likely to improve our own lives and those of other natural beings. The human being, although the product of hundreds of millions of years of selective evolution, is far from being a perfect creation. By the end of the millennium, human beings will very likely be different from human beings today.

What kind of world all this will produce depends partly on who these developments are intended to benefit. They hold out the prospect of an increasingly unequal world, with, as today, some people reaping the benefits of new technologies while others, who do not have access to them, fall further behind in material well-being. Indeed they hold new possibilities of inequality. There could be a self-perpetuating class divide between those whose parents could afford expensive pre-natal tailoring and those who turn out just as chance dictated. Some poor countries which today provide cheap labour for the rich world may one day breed cheap labourers, designed to be able to survive and work in inhospitable climes such as the polar regions. We will also have the power to do these things to reduce the immense amount of suffering that has always accompanied humankind's sojourn on this planet.

The fact of having these powers, like the ability to permeate the atmosphere with radioactivity or to change the climate, raises questions about our relationship to the rest of the natural world, and our rights and responsibilities with respect to it. Attitudes to this relationship are meta-political. They transcend politics. But they will influence policy decisions. Some attitudes are likely to be more helpful than others, although ultimately this is based on value judgements and therefore will always be a matter of opinion.

We should respect and value nature and natural processes. There is nothing mystical or sentimental about this. There are sound reasons why we should value natural processes and learn from them. Nature learns by trial and error, as Darwin explained to us. So do we. But nature has had more time than we have had to experiment, and try out different possibilities. Living organisms today are the product of hundreds of millions of years of trial and error.

There is an intelligence at work in some animals that we do not understand. Birds migrate annually over thousands of miles, navigating with an accuracy that we could not attain until the invention of the global positioning satellite. A baby sea turtle born on a beach in Florida sets out for the island of Ascension in the South Atlantic, 3000 miles away, floating south with the current. It spends most of its life there if it survives the journey, and then swims against the prevailing current back to the very same beach from which it set out, where it lays its eggs. No human sailor could achieve this. A beehive built as a series of hexagonal panels is so perfect a structure in maximizing space and durability that architects have only just created a mathematical model. A spider using pieces of dead insect manufactures a thread stronger than the material with which bullet-proof vests are made. A colony of South American ants numbers between one and three million and may occupy 3000 underground chambers; each member carries out its task to contribute to the successful operation of the colony.

We do not know of any biological process by which knowledge can be passed on to offspring. None the less, a baby bird which is hatched in isolation will still recognize a predator and take shelter. What kind of knowledge is passed on to us through the womb? The ability to use language, as many linguists believe? An instinct for numbers? Gender differences? We would like to know.

As we have seen, one reason for preserving biodiversity is to allow the natural process of evolution by Darwinian trial and error to continue in millions of species, to see what will develop.

Nature also has an aesthetic value for us. We seem to want other living things to share the world with us, living things that have a life of their own and that are not, like farm animals or domestic pets, there for our pleasure and convenience. We seem to have a need to experience an environment that is not of our choosing, that is larger and older than anything that we have created. We need them in the same way that we need to know who our ancestors are and where we come from. We need to encounter a mountain range, a vast, roaring ocean, a forest of mighty trees, things that cannot be subjected to our will. In this secular age when the notion of God is banished from most worldly affairs, we need something else to enable us to feel awe and humility.

The tension between respect for natural forces and the need to adapt them to our purposes will be characteristic of a world in which people are becoming more numerous, more demanding and more technically powerful.

We should be on the side of humankind. It is natural to be revolted sometimes at the havoc that people have wrought on the natural world, and it is healthy to prefer green things to grey and the field to the bulldozer. But this is an aesthetic reaction more than a moral one, and should not be allowed to topple over into permanent anger at one's own kind to the detriment of human sympathies.

Some environmentalists cast humankind as the villain in the drama of life, plundering and destroying with reckless abandon. The human race is 'an affliction on the world', wrote Thomas Berry in an article put out by the Sierra Club. 'The phenomenal expansion of human population that we are now seeing can be seen as clusters of cancer cells spreading to more areas of the Earth's surface', wrote Ralph Metzner in his book *Green Psychology*. This is not just favouring population control; this is the language of race hatred applied to the human race. The apotheosis of this attitude was the formation in Portland, Oregon in the early 1990s of the Voluntary Human Extinction Movement, which advocated phasing out the human race in order to save millions of animals and plants threatened by human activity.

'Deep ecologists' argue that every species has an equal right to exist, and that to favour the human one over others is 'specist'.

This position is pragmatically difficult to maintain and ethically dubious. The only moral values we have are human ones, which we do not share with other animals. We can ponder their rights. They cannot ponder ours.

Respect for other life-forms is an admirable guideline in behaviour but it should not override all other considerations. Between the farmer and the locust, our sympathies should be with the farmer. Yes, we should preserve biodiversity, but like other animals we have the right to defend ourselves against our enemies, using whatever tools we have. Not many mourn the passing of the smallpox virus.

The American ecologist and essayist John Muir counsels reverence for all life. He says we should not impose our standards of beauty and ugliness on other creatures such as snakes and alligators, for these deserve to be respected as much as other creatures that might seem prettier in our sight. This is respecting nature. But then he rhapsodizes to the alligators: 'Honourable representatives of the great saurians of older creation, may you long enjoy your lilies and rushes, and be blessed now and then with a terror-stricken man by way of a dainty.' Surprisingly, this cruel sentiment is quoted without disapproval in Bill McKibben's widely praised and generally humane book *The End of Nature*,[4] which shows the strange places to which reverence for all living things can lead.

Just as we should give due respect to the rest of nature, so we should give due respect to humankind. Humans have an intelligence that no other animal has. The navigational intelligence of birds, the extraordinary architectural intelligence of bees, are wonders to behold and to be studied, but they are programmed. They are narrow and limited in their functions.

Humankind can think broadly. We can look into the future and see consequences. We are a unique species. Ninety-nine per cent of the species that have ever existed have become extinct, so if humans were like other species, it would seem that we also, in the course of aeons, are doomed to extinction. But humans can understand the forces of nature and use this understanding to survive. We can make choices that other species cannot make. The human race may not become extinct. We should value its intelligence.

Humans have something else that is unique in nature and that also deserves to be valued: a moral sense, the ability to empathize with another creature's happiness or pain. This does not always guide our actions, any more than our ability to look ahead and see the consequences. Often we operate with the same motivation as other animals but with technological sophistication. Human beings are carnivores, but unlike other carnivores, when we kill other animals for food we make pigs and chickens live their lives in cramped prisons and torture geese to make pâté de foie gras. But people also choose to be kind to animals. They pass laws insisting that food animals be slaughtered humanely. They consider the welfare of other species, and even of one another. Other creatures do not.

Humans have the right to impose their moral values on the rest of nature because they are the only creatures with moral values. Who would not kill humanely an animal dying in pain of natural causes, or rescue from drowning an animal caught in a flood that is a part of a natural cycle?

The ability to change human beings fundamentally, if we acquire it, will provide new opportunities to impose our moral values on nature, and to improve on the natural development of the species. Nature is wise in caring for the continuation of the species, but brutally indifferent to the individual.

Pain is natural and necessary, the mechanism for warning an organism that something is wrong and corrective action needs to be taken. But the capacity for pain of a complex organism is far greater than needed. The cow dying of thirst in a drought would look for water even if its agony were only half as great. In the case of a human being, a still more complex organism with higher mental faculties, this capacity for pain is terrifying beyond imagining. If we were to apply human criteria to nature, we would say this is one of nature's mistakes. Perhaps we will learn to correct it. People have developed analgesics from the earliest times. Perhaps people will learn to intervene at a basic level and reduce species' capacity for pain.

Advances in biotechnology already bring closer one possibility of reducing suffering on a large scale. We may soon be able to produce meat that has never been a part of a living animal. The meat will be produced with proteins and carbohydrates from the animal's genetic material. We will be able to eat meat and fish without killing or imprisoning a living creature.[5] (There will be some traditionalists who will say that, like genetically modified organisms, this meat is not natural, and will insist that their roast leg of lamb will not taste the same unless some little creature gamboling in the fields has been killed to get it to them.)

If this were to become widespread, so that the practice of raising farm animals for meat became obsolete, then a huge amount of land would be released for growing food. Another consequence, quite possibly, would be that people would look back on the practice of keeping animals in cruel conditions and then killing them with horror and incomprehension, much as we look back on our forefathers' tolerance of slavery, now that we can enjoy the comforts they enjoyed without keeping slaves.

Since the Enlightenment, we have celebrated Promethean Man. Like the original Prometheus, who stole fire from the gods and gave it to mankind, he is daring, adventurous, challenging any limits placed upon him. Man's achievement, his glory even, lay in subduing nature. In the language used until recently to describe human progress, men 'conquered' the wilderness, 'tamed' rivers, and carved cities and roads out of virgin forests. He used his spirit and his intellect to bend nature to his will.

He was enjoined to do so. Francis Bacon, the 17th century British philosopher who pointed the way to experimental science, used a striking metaphor, saying that nature should be 'put to the question'. This term meant putting a criminal on the rack or some other torture implement and twisting his limbs until he yielded information.

The scientific enterprise was to enhance men's power over the rest of nature. René Descartes, another of the spiritual founders of modern science, wrote: 'It is possible to obtain knowledge by means of which, knowing the force and the action of fire, water, air, the stars and all other bodies that environ us . . . we can employ them in all those uses to which they are adapted, and thus render ourselves the masters and possessors of nature.'[6]

Scientific and technical achievements were welcomed universally. They represented progress. One only had to look around to see the benefits they brought, from antibiotics to air travel.

Americans in particular were supremely Promethean. They inherited a vast, thinly populated continent in which to build a new nation. America's heroes are the explorers and pioneers who transformed this wilderness into a home for civilization, carving paths through mountain ranges and townships out of forests. The attitude to an inhospitable landscape is seen in an account, probably apocryphal, that was quoted approvingly by American newspapers during World War Two, of an exchange with a Pacific islander. The islander said, 'Japanese fight well in jungle. British fight well in jungle. But when Americans come, jungle goes'.

Now Environmental Man has come along as our new role model. Environmental Man treads softly. He respects nature, reveres it even, and regrets the damage he has done to it. He tries to have as small an impact as possible. His aim is not to conquer nature but to live in harmony with it and adapt to its ways. He respects 'primitive' societies and the ways they have found to adapt to their environment as he respects other life forms.

Today things are deemed to be good because they are 'natural'. Products are sold on the basis of what they do not have. No additives, no preservatives, no artificial flavouring, no artificial colouring, as if poisons come only from laboratories and not from things that grow. But freshly picked toadstools are not healthier than frozen mushrooms.

Yes, Man must tread carefully, and watch where he is walking. Like some blundering colossus, he is in the habit of tripping over bits of the environment and breaking them. Environmental Man must guide Promethean Man. But he should not simply inhibit him. For we need Promethean Man also. Man is a part of nature, and it is part of his nature to create, to build, to explore. It is as natural for men to build a hydro-electric dam as it is for beavers to construct a log dam across a stream. We and the beavers are doing the same thing: adapting a part of the environment to suit our needs. A beaver uses its teeth and paws to change its surroundings, just as a bird uses its beak to build a nest and a fox its claws to dig a burrow. Man's most powerful organ, the one that has enabled him to dominate creatures that are stronger and faster, is his brain, and he uses his brain when he builds machines and utilizes sources of power beyond his own body.

A beaver dam changes its local environment but a hydro-electric dam changes it much more. Man has more power than other animals. In the course of making his life safer, more comfortable and richer, he can wreak havoc on a scale that no other animal can. That is why he must tread carefully. Fortunately, Man also has the intelligence to see what he is doing, or if not that, then to see what he has done, and correct it. We have become aware of our power as Promethean people, and of the damage that we have caused unwittingly to the land, the seas and the atmosphere, in which we live and on which we depend.

We must be cautious, but we are learning caution from some of our mistakes. Promethean Man tends towards hubris. Environmental Man tends towards timidity that can hold us back from using our potential. Intervening in the natural order will not mean substituting ourselves for it.

Perceptions of the environment and of relevant factors like our use of materials, economic growth and global inter-dependence, are changing. An appreciation of the fact that we can damage the natural world by what were once everyday activities is now wide-spread. Impacts on it are being factored into some industrial activities. We have responded to the realization of environmental degradation effectively in many cases. There is also reason for alarm. The changes we are making are little and late, and more and more people are demanding more and more material goods and services.

In taking action on climate change and other human impacts on the planetary environment, governments must act together and must do so not only for their own people but for all the world's people. When people speak up for action on climate change, they are doing so as citizens of the world as well as of their own country.

Looking at the slow pace at which change is taking place, but also at what can be done and is being done, one can look at the future with a certain amount of pessimism, but qualified by the knowledge that people in groups can act politically to better their collective lot, and the likelihood that eventually this will happen.

We don't have any choice about whether to intervene in the ecology of the planet. We are doing so. We have to direct our impact and sometimes reduce it; that is management. We also have to decide among ourselves who does what; that is politics.

APPENDIX

POLITICAL NEWS FROM A WARMER WORLD

Items from the US press in the year 2060

WASHINGTON, JANUARY 2 – Senator Travis Groves (Republican Party) will introduce a bill in the Senate authorizing the president to take military action against any country that emits more than 3 tonnes of carbon per capita into the atmosphere annually, he said today.

Senator Groves told a press conference in a prepared statement: 'I had prepared this bill for the eventuality that the UN conference on a new global quota system for carbon emissions would end in failure. Unhappily, that has now come to pass.'

'We in America have brought our emissions down to 3 tonnes per capita, and we are prepared to reduce them further as part of a commonly agreed international effort. We have shown that we are prepared to make efforts for the common good. All the international plans we have supported have included special arrangements for the developing countries. None the less, the effort must be shared.

'The insistence by a number of countries that the advanced industrialized countries accept almost all the burden is unacceptable, and shows a rigidity and an unwillingness to compromise that threatens to bring disaster to us all. We must now act unilaterally, if need be, to protect not only our own interests but those of the whole world.'

When a reporter pointed out that several countries, notably India and Brazil, are expected to reach that level in the next three years, Groves said only: 'I am aware of that fact.'

Another reporter asked whether this bill would mean that the United States would declare war on those countries if they exceed the 3-tonne limit. He said, 'My bill authorizes the president to take whatever action he deems appropriate at the time. It does not instruct'.

Another questioner took up this point. 'What do you envisage?' he asked. 'Do we invade an offending country? Do we bomb its coal-burning power plants?' The senator simply repeated that it would be up to the president to decide on appropriate action.

When a reporter asked whether other countries might not see this as aggression Groves became heated in his reply. 'What's aggression?' he demanded. 'It would be aggression if another country were to send warships to shell our coastal cities, wouldn't it? So isn't it aggression if countries burn coal irresponsibly so that our coastal cities are flooded and we have to build sea walls? Isn't it aggression when they cause our Midwest farms to dry up? Just as it would be if they dropped bacteria bombs on them? And isn't it aggression against countries that are suffering terrible famine because of these emissions?'

There was an immediate response from India. A statement issued through the Indian Embassy here said: 'It is to be hoped that the American Administration will reject immediately Senator Groves' proposal. It is nothing more than an attempt to impose by military means the unequal arrangements that have already proved unacceptable.'

HARARE, ZIMBABWE, MARCH 2 – The UN Disaster Relief Agency is closing shop. Today it issued its long-expected announcement that it is ceasing operations.

The announcement follows rejection by the major participating nations of a final request that they resume funding for the agency.

DRA director Joseph Nkimah called the decision 'a tragedy which will contribute to making this decade one of unprecedented suffering for the human race'.

The DRA has been winding down its activities for some time. Six months ago, it said it could no longer call on NATO's quick-reaction emergency relief force because of the unsettled question of who would pay the cost.

The DRA was created 14 years ago in an atmosphere of crisis and a spirit of goodwill. Despite complaints about a swollen bureaucracy, it has brought balm to some of the bleeding wounds of the planet.

Its fieldworkers, drawn from many countries, acquired a reputation for dedication and competence, whether distributing food to the starving in drought-stricken central Africa or the Ukraine, or mounting massive rescue operations for flood victims in Bangladesh or the Nile Delta. It has saved hundreds of thousands of lives, perhaps millions. It will not be saving any more.

The US government's rejection of the appeal for more funds was followed by similar rejections by the countries of the EU. The White House said in a statement today: 'We are facing unprecedented calls for help from areas of our own country suffering climatic damage. We regret the decision, but for the moment the needs of our own people must come first.'

The response of countries that have been the recipients of DRA aid has been bitter. A typical comment came from Bangladeshi prime minister Sami Rao: 'This decision is a renunciation of our common humanity. Our children and our children's children will remember it.'

PARIS, APRIL 4 – The French Foreign Ministry announced today that scientists at the Pasteur Institute in Paris have developed a new strain of salt-resistant rice.

This is expected to be of great value in those areas where rice farming has been hit by rising sea levels and the salination of the soil, such as Egypt, Bangladesh and the Yangtse Valley in China. These areas have experienced famine in recent years.

One of the Pasteur Institute scientists behind the discovery, Marc Tardieu, drew attention to an important feature of today's rice strain. He told a reporter: 'This requires less irrigation than normal rice. We regard this as crucially important because of the worldwide shortage of fresh water.'

The fact that the announcement comes from the Foreign Ministry underlines the political importance of the discovery for France. A reduction in irrigation for rice means a reduction of the amount of methane emitted in the cultivation. If this is proven it can be counted as part of France's contribution to the Climate Change Technology Transfer Program. This has been lagging behind the required figure, and brought a warning last month from the director of the program.

The deputy foreign minister, Yvonne Beuve-Marie, said seeds will be made available immediately to any country that wants them through the UN Food and Agriculture Organization. 'We anticipate that 100,000 acres will be restored to rice-growing within five years,' she said.

NEW ORLEANS, JUNE 1 – The largest procession ever seen in this city famous for its processions flowed down Decateur Street and filled Jackson Square today in a massive protest against the Federal Government's 30-year flood defense plan announced earlier this month.

The Mayor of New Orleans, the two Louisiana Senators, local Congressmen and other civic leaders led the procession, which included six marching jazz bands. But this was no Mardi Gras. The mood was one of angry defiance rather than revelry.

The first reaction here when the Government plan was announced was stunned shock. Now that it has dawned on the citizens of New Orleans that the Government really intends to abandon their city and the surrounding area to the floodwaters, the feeling is one of outrage. Letters to local newspapers have called for the impeachment of the president.

The civic outrage was given expression today in the oratory of Mayor Dean Boardman. Boardman, a plump, balding, bespectacled figure with florid features made redder by his emotion, addressed the crowd outside City Hall. He told them: 'The plan says that economic logic shows the country can't afford to protect the whole

Mississippi Delta from the rising level of the sea, that it makes more sense to put the money into flood defenses elsewhere where they are needed.'

'It says we are all to abandon our homes over the next 30 years. Money will be given to help us resettle. We are all – all of us – to become refugees. And President Nye is prepared to accept this plan. This is economic logic, we are told. When the whole of the American coastline is threatened, economic logic dictates that the Mississippi Delta must be given up.' Boardman pronounced the phrase 'economic logic' with impassioned scorn.

With his jowls shaking with indignation, he went on: 'It's a good thing that Andrew Jackson and not President Nye was in charge of the defense of this city when the British redcoats landed here in 1815. President Nye wouldn't have called in his sharpshooters and artillery. Oh no! He would have called in accountants and had them calculate the cost of defending the city. He might have decided that *economic logic* showed that it would be better to surrender, to run up a white flag.' There was more in this style, which the audience greeted with enthusiasm.

'I am convinced,' Boardman went on, 'that when the American people realize what is actually happening, and what can happen, they will refuse to sacrifice this great city, which is so much a part of America's history, whatever the cost. They will pay anything rather than tell a million of their fellow-Americans that they must give up their homes.'

There is no doubt that most New Orleans citizens share Boardman's anger. Local radio talk shows are full of bitter comments about the large sums being spent to build sea walls around Manhattan and Miami.

But most people are privately sceptical about the possibility of overturning the plan. The muted reaction of Congress has been noted here and it is not encouraging. One downtown saloon keeper, hearing a speaker on a radio phone-in talk of a new war between the states, snorted, 'That's crap. The War Between the States began when the Southern states seceded. Where are we going to secede to? The Gulf of Mexico?'

SWANAGE, ENGLAND, AUGUST 12 – This part of Britain's south coast is a new tourist boom area, bringing local prosperity and much-needed foreign currency into the British economy.

Once tourists came to Britain to see the sights and theater in London and the grandeur of the former royal palaces, or perhaps the literary landmarks of the Lake District and the misty crags of the Scottish Highlands.

Today sun and sand are a major attraction. Britain is attracting the sun-seeking vacationers who once flocked to Mediterranean resorts that are now baking in tropical heat and plagued by malaria. The change in the climate that has brought flooding and hardship to Britain's northeast has turned this part of the country into one of Europe's favorite vacation lands.

This looks like being the best year yet for Britain's seaside resorts. They expect five million visitors, at least half of them from abroad.

The Club Mediteranée outside this Dorset town is a good place to see the holiday boom. Pierre Dauphin, the club's manager, said: 'England is definitely our biggest growth area. This is the fifth Club Mediteranée village that we've opened in England and it's a great success. We're booked out until the end of September. People seem to be enjoying themselves here. Look at them.' He pointed to a sybaritic scene of people lying on the beach, swimming or heading up to lunch at the outdoor tables.

The attractions here are the same as those in other Club Mediteranée villages. The daytime temperature rarely falls below a comfortable 20 degrees centigrade, the wines from the local Dorset vineyards are good value, the palm-fringed village abuts on to a long, sandy beach and an orange grove makes a colorful backdrop.

Several towns along Britain's south coast are now on the jet-set's holiday map. Torquay with its casino is now favored by the European smart set, while Poole's principal attraction is its luxury yachting marina.

ROME, SEPTEMBER 14 – The terrorist group calling itself People's Defenders struck again last night, cutting off electricity to much of southern Europe. They sabotaged the solar power complex in the Sahara with two 100-pound bombs placed under two of the four giant reflectors.

People's Defenders said this was a response to the sinking by a EU frigate of another ship bringing intended migrants across the Mediterranean last week after the ship refused to turn back, with the loss of some 200 lives.

Many parts of Italy, Greece, Spain and Croatia were without regular light or heat. Dozens of deaths are reported already, some in small hospitals where there is no emergency generator. Most airports are closed and many rail services halted.

The Sahara complex, at Bani Walid, Libya supplies 45 per cent of the electricity to these four European countries. Drivers in these countries are asked not to take their cars on the roads unless absolutely necessary. Even where the traffic lights are operating, the authorities say the strain on power supplies means they cannot be guaranteed to stay on. In Spain the government has put into operation an emergency rationing system, cutting off electricity for all but emergency services for 12 hours a day in blocks of two hours. Here in Italy the Pope has cancelled his planned television address this evening because transmission cannot be guaranteed.

People's Defenders, the terrorist group that claims to speak for the deprived people of the developing world, announced its responsibility for the attack immediately in a statement issued to news agencies. It promised more actions unless the Western countries change their policies. 'The people who drowned on the *Omar* last week are only the latest victims of Western policies on greenhouse gases,' the announcement said. 'Millions of people have died and are dying in Africa so that the citizens of Western countries can continue to have a lifestyle of affluence. We will ensure that they do not die in silence.'

European Union security director Sean Garrity told reporters that an investigation is under way to determine how terrorists penetrated the security cordon around the solar power complex. Asked by a reporter whether he has any more information on the rumors that People's Defenders has assembled bacteriological weapons, he said, 'I can only repeat what I said last week: unfortunately, the possibility cannot be ruled out.'

In Brussels, the European Immigration Office said it does not contemplate changing its policy on immigration despite the desperate conditions in parts of Africa. It repeated its earlier statement that the deaths on the *Omar* were tragic, but the responsibility lay with those who sent the ship.

Demonstrations against the policy continued in several European capitals. In Brussels, a group from Lifeboat International sat throughout the day opposite the European Commission building with placards accusing it of genocide.

OTTAWA, OCTOBER 28 – The Canadian government today announced new border restrictions on travelers coming from the United States. Short-stay permits will be abolished and anyone wanting to stay for more than two weeks will require a visa.

The move is aimed at illegal immigration from America, and follows last month's announcement of a new quota on American immigration.

Canadian immigration minister Roy Bridges acknowledged in a statement that the new restrictions might impede commerce and tourism, but insisted that they are necessary.

'Four million Americans have come into Canada in the last 15 years, and they have become loyal Canadians and contributed to our society and our prosperity,' he said. 'But our economy cannot take any more at this time. Also, we wish to maintain a balance in our social make-up, and to continue to take in immigrants from Britain and from continental Europe.'

Coincidentally, the announcement came on the same day as publication of a study by the sociology department of McGill University in Montreal of the pattern of American immigration. The study showed that the numbers passed the 400,000-annually mark in 2038, which was the year that Canada's GNP overtook America's.

The majority of Americans came from the barren parts of what was once the Midwest farm belt and from the sweltering, disease-prone cities of the South. At first they tended to move up to Canada's prairie provinces, and particularly to the new northern areas that opened up to farming as the permafrost melted, but in recent years they have gone to all parts of Canada.

NEW YORK, DECEMBER 4 – UN secretary-general Kao Yamagishi announced today that he is convening another conference on global climate measures, raising hopes of a new agreement on greenhouse gas emissions.

Yamagishi said several developments since the failure of the last conference earlier this year give grounds for optimism. Officials of the major powers have been talking privately, and new compromise schemes have been discussed.

'All nations appreciate fully the urgency of the situation, and the consequences of continued international anarchy in this area,' the secretary-general said.

Sources close to the Secretariat said the basis of the hoped-for new agreement will be the German–Korean–Indian plan for an agreed reduction of greenhouse gas emissions according to a complicated formula based on population, needs and past performance. The formula includes all the principal greenhouse gases as well as carbon dioxide.

Joint implementation schemes will feature in it, and so will reforestation, paving the way for the huge EU–Brazil–Colombia scheme, which has been temporarily shelved.

Major Western governments welcomed Yamagishi's announcement and said they would work for a new agreement.

Notes

Introduction

1 Meadows et al, 1992
2 Rifkin, 1992

1 Midgley's Children

1 Gore, 1992
2 From the poem *Pity this busy monster* by e e cummings
3 A report produced for the Stockholm International Peace Research Institute in 1975 calculated that nuclear tests have caused 150,000 early deaths from cancer worldwide
4 *A Thousand Days* by Arthur Schlessinger, André Deutsch, London 1965
5 Benedick, 1991
6 ibid
7 Hardin and Baden, 1997
8 A typical prisoners' dilemma scenario goes like this. Two men are arrested for a crime and kept apart. Each is told: 'If neither of you confesses, you will both get a two-year sentence. But if

one of you confesses and implicates the other, he will get a one-year sentence and the other will get five years.' If they could collaborate, they would agree to say nothing. But each does not know that the other will not implicate him to get a lighter sentence so he may implicate the other first

9   Mohammed Ilyas in *Effects of Changes in Stratospheric Ozone and Global Climate* edited by JG Titus, UNEP, 1997

2 THE CLIMATE OF THE TIMES

1   *Security Studies and Power Politics,* article in *International Affairs,* October 1998
2   IPCC, Second Assessment, 1995, vol 1
3   *Climate Change from an Antarctic Perspective,* a paper put out on the British Antarctic Survey website
4   *New Scientist*, September 4, 1999
5   McConnell, 1996
6   RIIA Briefing Paper No 32, *The IPCC Second Assessment Report,* July 1966

3 WHO DOES WHAT?

1   From the poem *Once by the Pacific*
2   Quoted by Fred Pearce in an article in *New Scientist*, November 13, 1998
3   *Climate Change and its Impacts,* Department of Transport and the Environment, UK, November 1998
4   Article in *Nature*, February 12, 1996
5   *Rapid Change in Past Climates,* paper by Jean Jouzel and Jean-Claude Duplessy, paper presented at the conference

The words quoted are the authors'. The meticulous reader will note that an event cannot be both 'multiple' and 'unprecedented'; only the first occurrence can be unprecedented

6   *Variability and Transitions of the Thermohaline Circulation* by R Saravanan and R Wood, paper presented at the conference

7   *Proceedings of the National Academy of Sciences,* April 1999

8   In an interview with the author

9   *The Guardian,* London, December 14, 1996

4   SOME NITTY-GRITTY

1   Essay in *International Regimes,* edited by Stephen Krasner, Cornell University Press, 1983. Quoted in Rowlands, 1995

2   *The Greenhouse Effect: Formulating a Convention,* Royal Institute of International Affairs paper, London 1990. William Nitze was a State Department negotiator on climate change under the Bush Administration but resigned because he disagreed with the administration's negative position. President Clinton appointed him to a senior EPA position

3   Benedick, 1991

4   Tickell, 1988

5   *The Greening of Machiavelli* by Tony Brenton, Royal Institute of International Affairs and Earthscan, London, 1996

6   *Earth in the Balance* by Al Gore, Earthscan, London, 1992

7   The reference is to President Kennedy's declaration of solidarity with West Berliners when they were threatened by East German pressure during the Cold War: 'Today we can say, "*Ich bin ein Berliner*".'

8   Quoted in Grubb and Vroljik, 1999

9   Grubb, 1990

10   It would be unfair to Michael Grubb not to say also that he
has since done valuable work for the IPCC and has helped
devise the carbon emission trading schemes that are currently
under consideration

5 What Price the World?

1   *Penguin Island* by Anatole France, translated by AW Evans,
John Lane, New York, 1909
2   In the magazine *Across the Board,* June 1978. Cited in *The Official
Rules* by Paul Dickson, Arrow Books, London, 1990
3   Nordhaus, 1994
4   Quoted in IPCC 1995 report, Working Group 3, Chapter 4
5   Broome, 1992
6   Fankhauser, 1995
7   Cairncross, 1995
8   In an article *Valuing Climate Change* in the journal *Chemistry
and Industry*, London, December 18, 1995
9   Cairncross, 1990
10   *Against the Gods: the Remarkable Story of Risk* by Peter L
Bernstein, John Wiley and Sons, New York, 1996
11   Wilson, 1998
12   Leakey and Lewin, 1995
13   ibid
14   *Nature,* September 23, 1999

6 Some More Nitty-gritty

1   *Democracy in America,* first published 1835, edited by Richard
D Heffner, Mentor Books, New York, 1955

2   *The Guardian*, October 29, 1998
3   Forsyth, 1999

7 NEW WAYS OF DOING THINGS

1   Grubb, 1990
2   *The Insolent Chariots* by John Cresswell Keats, Fawcett Publications, Greenwich, Connecticut, 1964
3   *Global Environment Outlook 2000*, United Nations Environment Programme, Earthscan, London, 1999
4   von Weizsäcker, Lovins and Lovins, 1998
5   Lovins, 1977
6   *Making Sense and Making Money,* Rocky Mountain Institute paper, 1998
7   Hawken, Lovins and Lovins, 1999
8   Article by Joseph Romm in *Atlantic Monthly*, April 1996
9   In the West, that is. Coal has been used in China for a thousand years – Marco Polo remarked on the 'black stones' that they burned – but it did not fuel an industrial revolution there
10 'The New Petroleum' by Richard Lugar and R James Wolsey, *Foreign Policy*, Jan–Feb 1999. President Clinton referred to it in a speech about energy and told his audience, 'If you haven't read it you should'.

8 NEAR FUTURE, FAR FUTURE

1   *What is History* by EH Carr, Penguin Books, London, 1964
2   *Social Theory and the Environment* by David Goldblatt, Polity Press, London, 1996
3   op cit, Chapter 7, note 3

4   *The End of Nature* by Bill McKibben, Anchor Books, New York, 1990
5   This is suggested by Gregg Easterbrook in his book *A Moment on Earth*, Penguin Books, London, 1995
6   *Discourse on Method, Part 6.* Quoted in *The Making of the Modern Mind* by John Hammond Randall, Houghton Mifflin, New York, 1940

BIBLIOGRAPHY

Adamson, David, *Defending the World*, I B Taurus, London, 1990

Benedick, Richard, *Ozone Diplomacy*, Harvard University Press, 1991

Broome, John, *Counting the Cost of Global Warming*, White Horse Press, Cambridge, Mass, 1992

Brown, Lester and others, *State of the World, 1999*, Worldwatch Institute, Washington D C, 1999. Also *State of the World, 1996, 1997, 1998*

Brown, Neville, *The Strategic Revolution*, Brassey's London, 1992

Brown, Paul, *Global Warming: Can Civilization Survive?* Blandford, London, 1996

Cairncross, Frances, *Costing the Earth,* Earthscan, London, 1990

Cairncross, Frances, *Green Inc.: a Guide to Business and the Environment,* Earthscan, London, 1995

Cline, William R, *The Economics of Global Warming* Institute for International Economics, Washington D C, 1992

Easterbrook, Gregg, *A Moment on the Earth: the Coming Age of Environmental Optimism,* Penguin Books, London, 1995

Fankhauser, Samuel, *Valuing Climate Change: the Economics of the Greenhouse,* Earthscan, London, 1995

Forsyth, Tim, *International Investment and Climate Change*, Earthscan, London, 1999

Gelbspan, Ross, *The Heat is On: the High Stakes Battle Over Earth's Threatened Climate,* Addison-Wesley, Reading, MA, 1997

Gore, Al, *Earth in the Balance*, Earthscan, London, 1992

Grubb, Michael, *Energy Policies and the Greenhouse Effect*, Royal Institute of International Affairs, London, 1990

Grubb, Michael, *The Greenhouse Effect: Negotiating Targets*, Royal Institute of International Affairs, London, 1992

Grubb, Michael, with Christian Vrolijk and Duncan Brack, *The Kyoto Protocol: a Guide and Assessment,* Royal Institute of International Affairs and Earthscan, London, 1999

Hardin, Garrett and John Baden, *Managing the Commons*, W H Freeman, San Francisco, 1997

Hawken, Paul, Amory B Lovins and L Hunter Lovins, *Natural Capitalism*, Earthscan, London, 1999

Held, David, *Democracy and the Global Order*, Polity Press, Cambridge, 1995

Houghton, John, *Global Warming: the Complete Briefing*, Lion Press, Oxford, 1994

Intergovernmental Panel on Climate Change, *Climate Change Reports*, Cambridge University Press, 1990, 1992, 1995

Kennedy, Paul, *Preparing for the Twenty-First Century*, Harper-Collins, London, 1993

Leakey, Richard and Roger Lewin, *The Sixth Extinction*, Doubleday, New York, 1995

Leggett, Jeremy, *The Carbon War: Dispatches from the End of the Oil Century*, Allen Lane, Penguin, London, 1999

Lovins, Amory B, *Soft Energy Paths Towards a Durable Peace*, Ballinger, Cambridge, MA, 1977

McConnell, Fiona, *The Biodiversity Convention: a Negotiating History,* Kluwer Law International, Boston, 1996

McNeil, Tim and others, *Beyond Interdependence,* Oxford University Press, Oxford, 1998

Meadows, Donella H, Dennis Meadows and Jorgen Randers, *Beyond the Limits,* Earthscan, London, 1992

Moss, Stephen and Paul Simons, *Weather Watch,* BBC Books, London, 1992

Nordhaus, William, *Managing the Global Commons: the Economics of Climate Change,* M.I.T. Press, Cambridge, Mass, 1994

Pearce, Fred, *Turning Up the Heat,* Bodley Head, London, 1989

Ponting, Clive, *A Green History of the World,* Penguin, London, 1994

Prins, Gwyn, ed *Threats Without Enemies,* Earthscan, London, 1993

Rifkin, Jeremy, *Confessions of a Heretic,* Simon and Schuster, New York, 1992

Rowlands, Ian H, *The Politics of Global Atmospheric Change,* Manchester University Press, Manchester, 1995

Schneider, Stephen, *Global Warming,* Lutterworth, London, 1990

Tickell, Sir Crispin, *The Influence of Climate Change on History,* Harvard University Press, Cambridge, Mass, 1988

Vogler, John, *The Global Commons: a Regime Analysis,* Wiley, London, 1995

von Weizsacker, Ernst, *Earth Politics,* Zed Books, London, 1994

von Weizsäcker, Ernst, Amory B Lovins and L Hunter Lovins, *Factor Four: Doubling Wealth, Halving Resource Use,* Earthscan, London, 1998

Wilson, Edward O, *Biophilia,* Harvard University Press, Cambridge, Mass, 1998

ACRONYMS AND
ABBREVIATIONS

AOSIS	Association of Small Island States
ATM	automated teller machine
CFC	chlorofluorocarbon
EPA	Environmental Protection Agency
GCC	Global Climate Coalition
GEF	Global Environment Facility
HCFC	hydrochlorofluorocarbon
HFC	hydrofluorocarbon
IPCC	Intergovernmental Panel on Climate Change
JUSCANZ	alliance of Japan, United States, Canada, Australia and New Zealand
NASA	National Aeronautics and Space Administration
NGO	non-governmental organization
ODP	ozone depleting potential
OECD	Organization for Economic Cooperation and Development
OPEC	Organization of Petroleum Exporting Countries
PV	photovoltaic cell
UNEP	United Nations Environment Programme
UV	ultraviolet
WMO	World Meteorological Organization
WTO	World Trade Organization

INDEX

CFCs (chlorofluorocarbons),
    invention, 4; uses of, 12;
    action against, 14–27;
    smuggling, 25–6, 40, 41,
    42, 54, 78, 94, 174
channel tunnel, 116
Chernobyl, 155
Chevron, 84
Chile, 16
China, and CFC agreement,
    24, 25; effects of climate
    change, 55; carbon
    emissions, 68–69;
    potential damage to, 105,
    108, 110, 134, 136–139;
    reducing emissions, 141,
    142, 157, 166, 198
Christian Aid, 68
Chrysler Corporation, 84
Clean Development
    Mechanism, 95, 96, 126,
    127, 141, 174
Climate Action Network, 81
Climate Change Levy, 130
Cline, William R, 114
Clinton, President Bill, 78, 82,
    84, 85; and Kyoto
    meeting, 93, 121; signs
    Kyoto Protocol, 126, 163
Club Mediteranée, 201
Club of Rome, 10

Concorde, 11, 116, 129
Conference on Environment
    and Development, 50,
    69–75, 85
consciousness, new forms, 184
Convention on Biodiversity,
    120–21, 123, 172
COP 1 (Conference of the
    Parties), Berlin, 81–84
COP 2, Geneva, 85
COP 3, Kyoto, 92–97
COP 4, Buenos Aires, 124
cost-benefit analysis, 102–5
Costa Rica, 87
cummings, e e, 1
Curitiba, Brazil, 162
Cyprus, 72

Darman, Richard, US Budget
    Director, 22
Darwin, Charles, 186
Dasgupta, Chandra, 71
Denmark, 128; and wind
    power, 157, 164
Descartes, René, 192
de Toqueville, Alexis, 124
de Montfort University, 152
Dickson, Paul, 209
discount rate, 103–5
DNA, 184
Domack, Gene, 34

implementation, 86; and
Kyoto meeting, 92–97;
and potential damage,
105–6, 125–6; and Kyoto
target, 127–29, 133, 136;
energy efficiency, 151;
and car ownership, 161
US Department of Energy,
101, 156
US Environmental Protection
Agency, 23, 24, 107
US National Academy of
Sciences, 45
US National Climate Data
Center, 32
US Senate, 79, 121, 125, 126,
170–71

value-of-life argument, 108–11
Vienna Convention, 15, 17
Vikings, 30
Voluntary Human Extinction
Movement, 188

Wall Street Journal, 90, 153
Wallace, John, 159
water shortage, iii, 174

Watson, Bob, 15, 16, 18
wave power, 158
Westphalia, Treaty of, 176–7
Widalsky, A, 103
Wilson, Edward O, 117
wind power, 139, 148, 150,
156–7
Wirth, Timothy, 82
Wolsey, R James, 210
Wood, R, 108
World Bank, 75, 135, 142
World Conservation Union,
117
World Health Organization,
13, 33, 136
World Skiing Championships,
33
World Meteorological Organi-
zation, 26, 32, 36, 49
World Resources Institute, 84,
131
World Trade Organization,
177, 178
World War Two, 52, 78, 192
Worldwatch, 140

Zimbabwe, 76, 197